S0-AYC-558

ICONIC COMMUNICATION

ICONIC COMMUNICATION
an annotated bibliography

W. H. Huggins and Doris R. Entwisle

The Johns Hopkins University Press
Baltimore and London

This work was supported by the
Office of Computing Activities GJ-336
National Science Foundation
Under Grant GJ-336

Manufactured in the United States of America

The Johns Hopkins University Press, Baltimore, Maryland 21218
The Johns Hopkins University Press Ltd., London

Library of Congress Catalog Card Number 73-8130
ISBN 0-8018-1528-2

Library of Congress Cataloging in Publication data
will be found on the last printed page of this book.

TABLE OF CONTENTS

PREFACE

Starting in the academic year 1965-66, we began research connected with computer-generated films. Although some of our interest has centered about the means--special computer languages--for generating such films,it has been evident from the beginning of our work that the most important problems concern how these films communicate visual messages to human beings (iconic communication). Computer graphics occupies an important position in the field of computer science today, but almost without exception in those activities of which we are aware, attention has been focused on the technical problems of software and hardware and not on the communicative act with the human being. In an effort to deal with iconic-communication problems we have assembled this annotated bibliography. It pulls together relevant information from perception, psychology, social anthropology, education, computer graphics, and other relevant areas. These references came to our attention as we tried to isolate and focus on problems in iconic communication that arose in our study of computer-generated films.

We are interested in how visual images, particularly those composed of certain shapes which move and change, may communicate information to human beings, especially quantitative, organized information of a technical or scientific sort. Few workers in computer-generated films have exhibited this concern. Even traditional films for displaying abstract ideas, for which computer animation is so appropriate, have been created entirely by intuitive means. A film maker, who may or may not be a technical expert in some fields, contrives sequences of images on the basis of his prior experience and intuition. In so far as we have been able to determine, he has no theoretical base to start from. If one film is successful, he may try to copy some aspects of that film in the future, but he is largely unable to account explicitly for viewer-effects in terms of the microstructures of the film--what specific cognitive changes were produced by what image, or why; what sequences are optimal or desirable; what timing is best, and the like. More knowledge about the principles of iconic communication is needed before these problems in application can be addressed by the growing numbers of persons who will be using the new technological media for visual communication.

The ability to generate moving pictorial images by computers is a feature of these remarkable devices that has been neglected until recently. The ability now available to portray concepts via moving images and symbols of a radically new genre represents a real breakthrough in "notation" but, so far, the potential in this new development remains largely unexplored along the dimensions of interest to us. There are several reasons for this.

Among these reasons are the lack of development of appropriate hardware and software for producing visual imagery easily and inexpensively; computer technology has been dominated by persons who seem to be happy with a simple, very limited alphabet of characters used to produce linear strings of symbols, and only in the past several years are graphic terminals becoming commonplace. Also, the interests and objectives of those who design and build this elaborate equipment are quite different from, say, the educator who is primarily concerned with communicating concepts. Furthermore, these concepts are likely to be expressed traditionally in the static symbolic forms of natural language or mathematics, and to invent new modes of expressing these concepts by dynamic visual imagery is tantamount to creating a new language to replace the old--a difficult undertaking that must surely meet resistance because it is unconventional and of little use to those who have already acquired symbolic literacy. Yet, the need to explore this potential is great and offers many challenging topics for research. We hope that this bibliography will cause others to join us in the exploration of what we see as the basic issues in iconic communication.

Many associates helped us assemble this bibliography. Beginning in September 1969, W. H. Huggins conducted a seminar on this topic for three years. Participating in the seminar were faculty, graduate students and undergraduate students of The Johns Hopkins University. This seminar, through its discussions and abstracting of papers, served both to clarify our thinking and expand the list of relevant bibliographic items. We are especially indebted to David Mishelevich who participated vigorously in the seminar for two years and who started this bibliography. Others who contributed to the preparation of this material in computer-readable form are Nicholas Beser, Barbara Bricks, Gaither Davis, John Bender, Judy Kennedy and Linda Olson. The names of the many persons who prepared the bibliographic items are listed in the beginning of that section. We also express our appreciation to John Lehmann of the National Science Foundation, who through Grant GJ-336, offered patient and sympathetic encouragement in our efforts to explore the various dimensions of this subject.

ICONIC COMMUNICATION

I. ICONIC COMMUNICATION

Iconic communication deals mainly with non-verbal communication between human beings by the use of visual signs and representations (such as pictures) that stand for an idea by virtue of a resemblance or analogy to it in contrast to symbolic communications where the meaning of a symbol is entirely nominal (such as English text describing a picture).

Pictures are understood universally. They can be used with young children or with adults who speak another language. The word "iconic," from the Greek ikon, implies a mode of communication using primitive visual imagery that relies on the ability of people to perceive natural form, shape and motion rather than on alphabetic symbols which are defined in terms of arbitrary conventions and which require special education to interpret. Human preoccupation with the verbal mode of communication is no doubt an important consequence of human anatomy. All human beings have organs to receive auditory stimuli (eg ears) and they have as well organs to produce such stimuli (eg voice boxes). Visual symbols and messages, by contrast, although received via the eyes, have not been generated easily and rapidly by human beings until recently -- human beings have no organ for rapid production of visual information analogous to the vocalic mechanisms for generating acoustic information.

The human body can generate visual information directly through gestures and motions. This is a kind of "silent language" capable of communicating feeling and emotion but incapable of expressing precise structural relationships. Instead, one must resort to drawing or painting, a skill that few humans possess and that is not very useful for communication because it is so time-consuming. There is a curious asymmetry, then, between our abilities to create and to perceive symbolic acoustic messages on the one hand, and our ability to perceive, but our inability to create, iconic visual messages on the other hand.

From the earliest days of infancy, humans respond to and process large amounts of visual information present in the natural environment. Over his first two years the child apparently lays down an enormous store of structural information about the 3-dimensional world in which he lives. He correlates spatial information with kinesthetic and haptic information (information gained through motion of the body and the sense of touch), and becomes an efficient receiver and processor of this spatially structured iconic information. But for most human beings this remains a one-sided affair. Very few human beings ever generate iconic information beyond that produced by manipulation of familiar objects and events in the natural world about them. The novel production of new forms exhibited by natural language seems largely missing except in a few individuals called "artists."

Let us note specific ways in which iconic communication is one-sided. No person rearranges directly the visual information that a second person perceives. For instance, the landscapes or views of interiors seen by a second person cannot be readily communicated to or altered by a first person. Contrast this with the way in which one human produces and rearranges symbolic information, or edits it, so that it will be optimally communicated to another. People alter their speech according to the characteristics of a listener, but more important they create communications by speaking and by encoding speech onto paper. Most people create symbolic messages--written text--for consumption by other persons, but few human beings create iconic messages. Excepting a handful of artists and animators, human beings are primarily consumers and not producers of iconic information.

Our thesis is that the new technology for producing graphic images will increasingly be used to create visual information not previously present in the natural environment. For the first time, iconic communication can occur where one human being produces dynamic visual symbols to communicate with other human beings. This new power of icon generation leads to interest in, and need for, a science of icon structure and sequencing in analogy with the science of linguistics which deals with the structure and sequencing of verbal information to convey meaning.

To expand on the need for a science of iconics, imagine that until now verbal messages were broadcast and heard by listeners capable of understanding and reproducing them, but that the broadcasting forces were not under human control. Imagine further that the listeners were unable to speak and so create their own verbal messages directly. Instead, the only other verbal messages available besides the broadcasts were verbal messages built up by compiling sentences or paragraphs presented in the broadcasts--some "books" exist that have been constructed by taking chunks from broadcasts. (These books are the analogs of present-day films or other kinds of visual messages produced photographically where visual information already in existence is reproduced and rearranged.) Only some of the broadcasts can be excerpted and put together to form verbal messages. No one has available the basic elements (letters or morphemes) or rules to use so that letters and words can be combined into meaningful verbal communications.

What has just been described as the hypothetical state of verbal messages is representative of the present state of affairs for visual messages. The views of natural events and the world around us are seen by us but we have no essential part in creating or altering these views. We have sequences of film produced by arranging views already in existence (like the "books' mentioned above made from chunks of broadcasts), but we can not, except if we are producers of computer-generated film or animators, generate visual messages ab initio. In fact there exists no theory or rationale suggesting how to start from the primitive elements of visual information--lines, geometric forms, images of objects, and the like--to produce iconic messages. We do not even know how to pick the primitive elements.

Until well into the present century, iconic messages--films, paintings, and the like--communicated relatively little information to any large portion of the population. TV and computer generated images have changed this. The number of persons who can generate images is rapidly increasing, but more important the total volume of images per creator is greatly amplified. Thus almost everyone, for the first time in history, is now viewing iconic communications that have been produced by other persons.

From this discussion, it is evident that the study of Iconic Communication impinges on many traditional disciplines. This feature has made the selection of the bibliography items given later in this book a rather arbitrary undertaking because each of the traditional disciplines itself has an enormous bibliography. Yet it was necessary to limit and restrict attention to those items having "iconic" content. This we have tried to do by employing a selective process best suggested by the Venn diagram shown in Fig. I-1.

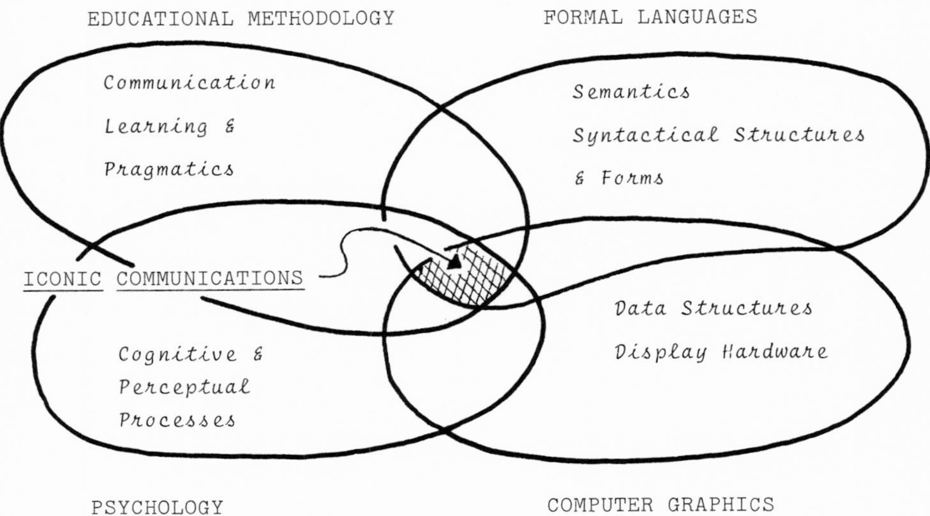

Figure I-1. The Field of Iconics.

Thus, iconics is concerned with that body of knowledge which in some sense is common to art and esthetics, cognitive and perceptual psychology, education and learning, linguistics and semantics, and computer graphics. The references included in the bibliography have had content in at least some of these different areas. Because of the enormous corpus of references associated with these various areas, our selection obviously cannot be exhaustive. Rather this bibliography is a sampling of work which we hope will be useful to others who are working in each of these different areas. Defined in this way, Iconics represents a bridge between these disciplines, with an emphasis on the human-oriented aspects, rather than on computer-science. In the following chapters, we shall examine in detail the relationships with some of these disciplines.

II. ICONICS AND EVOLUTION

A few words are needed about the concept of imagery (see also Chapter VI). We define imagery as a mental process of generating or registering visual images. Iconic communication proceeds by way of visual images. Although visual images may be realized as after-images, eidetic images, memory images, or imagination images (see RICHARDSON 1969), we are less concerned with the psychological realization than with the external process, the iconic message, that gives rise to the images. We are concerned with what features of the iconic message are tuned to cognitive functioning, with what parts of the message are processed to yield "iconic information," and especially with what makes a "memorable" image.

Like Gibson (1969) we see perception as "extracting information from stimulation." Stimulation emanates from the world around us and it carries information about that world--it specifies the world. "Perception" then means extracting information about the world from sensory stimulation. Gibson divides visual perception into that involving space and events in space and that involving objects and permanent items like written letters. The first is processed by way of ambient vision (at any instant an extensive portion of the visual space around the body is mapped) and the second, by way of focal vision (at any instant its scope is restricted but it can be extended over time by sampling movements of the eyes). Discrimination of events in space is primitive. Discrimination of fine-grain objects and patterns is a more recent adaptive achievement in evolutionary development. Reading of letters and words, a highly developed learned visual activity, depends largely on focal vision. (However, the remarkable skill of speed readers suggests that the scope of focal vision may be extended by training.) Processing of letters and words in written materials depends entirely on complex learnings built up as a consequence of formal instruction. Processing of an iconic image, on the other hand, depends both on the primitive information processing skills characteristic of ambient vision and on the use of focal vision to register details of images where the meaning is not of the arbitrary sort found in letters and words. Some images, in other words, are small enough to require focal vision but their iconic properties are such that cognitive processing does not depend on complex learnings applied to printed messages.

Because an iconic image has a basic resemblance to the object it is intended to specify, processing probably depends much less on formal learning than the processing of alphabetic and numeric information that is both language- and culture-specific. Any human being anywhere in the world without much training can understand a movie showing himself and his fellows moving about over the ground. The comprehension of spatial relationships and of motion among objects modelled closely after those seen in the real world does not require formal education. Iconic imagery makes use of such spatial relationships and motion. So far at least, it depends little on arbitrary conventions and patterns but rather utilizes the structural properties manifest in the natural world.

An iconic message is apprehended by means of parallel processing. Pictures and patterns in pictures are processed as complete unities, not in some fixed sequence like a line of print. Alphabetic information and language consist of sequential elements organized in linear strings. Information in an alphabetic message derives from the position of the ordered elements in the linear string as well as from the particular elements used. Thus "tip" and "pit" contain the same three elements, but the arrangement of the elements produces a different message. The elements in iconic messages are not constrained to linear strings but are organized in a multidimensional space, and the interrelations between the elements are therefore enormously more complex and rich. Because what is seen by the viewer depends upon his own vantage point in this same space, properties of invariance associated with geometrical transformations of translation, rotation and reflection and perspective take on a significance that is lacking in linear strings. For instance, in viewing a triangle the resulting image yields the same iconic message irrespective of whether the viewer focuses on one vertex (A) and then the others (B,C) or starts at (B) or (C). In fact, there is reason to believe that the whole triangle may be viewed and processed as a unit, much the way a landscape is seen. On the other hand, a number of possible spatial arrangements of the three points are possible, and the locus of the points is not limited to sequential rearrangments like ABC, BAC, and so on. The spatial deployment of the three points in some two-space vastly increases the potential information available, because one triangle out of a very large set of triangles is presented. If (A) and (B) are fixed we can move (C) to produce many shapes and sizes of triangles. The information is potentially very rich, but parallel processing (EGETH 1973) allows the information to be rapidly and easily encoded despite its richness.

Human beings as a species have evolved so their ability to process iconic messages is highly developed. Persons, rabbits, or cockroaches find their way around in a complex visual world. A young child once having entered a school on the ground floor, climbed stairs to another floor, and then proceeded down a corridor to a classroom, can find his way back out of the school or repeat the process on entering the next day. In fact, a young child can accurately follow a complicated path to and from school without being able to direct verbally another person how to do so. This ability to orient in space and to travel about must depend on the registering of visual images and upon the ability to call the pertinent images up for review when needed without interference from other, perhaps quite similar, images stored on other occasions. The ability to find one's way about, largely taken for granted, is actually quite remarkable. Exceptions to this are noted as in a desert where the iconic messages from the landscape are all alike. Only under exceptional circumstances--a first visit to a city--do people resort to conceptual crutches like maps. People remember their way around cities they have not seen for years and never expect to see again.

Evidence is mounting (ENTWISLE and HUGGINS 1973; FEINMAN and ENTWISLE 1972; HABER 1970; KAGAN 1970) that the capacity for processing iconic information exists in amounts and for time periods that are truly astounding. First-grade children, for example, can recognize almost perfectly large numbers of landscapes and cityscapes they have seen for only a few seconds a week earlier (ENTWISLE and HUGGINS 1973). These scenes were not familiar, they were complex, and they were shown under the most casual conditions. There apparently exists an enormous facility for processing, storing, and recognizing previously seen iconic information of the kind commonly found in human environments. This facility develops naturally without special tutelage. Kagan (1970) suggests that this facility also extends to pictures of objects like lathes or slide rules that children have never seen before and cannot even name, (although they may recognize familiar shapes and relationships in the subparts of the object).

Even though we know very little about iconic messages, the ability of human beings to deal efficiently with large amounts of iconic data offers exciting possibilities in the service of education.

III. RELATION OF ICONICS TO LINGUISTICS

The possiblity of a science upon which to base iconic communication may at first seem strange. It will help in considering the need for a science of iconics to review very briefly the present state of linguistics.

There is no human group presently known which does not have a grammatical language. A grammar, in its formal sense, describes explicitly the abstract self-contained system of rules that govern how persons generate sentences and communicate with one another. The rules are not simple. Indeed complete transformational grammars, which contain the proper set of transformations to mediate between the deep and surface structure of a language so that all grammatical sentences of a language (and only those) are derived, are yet not realized. An example of two sentences whose surface structures look alike but whose deep structures differ shows how difficult the problem is. "John is eager to please." vs "John is easy to please." Linguistics grapples with the problems of stating rules to govern such sentences.

It should be understood that so-called "primitive" peoples have languages that are in no way primitive, simple, nor underdeveloped. There appears to be no correlation between the relative complexity of a language and other aspects of human culture. Also, people who speak a language can use it for communication while closely obeying a complex set of rules without necessarily being aware of the existence of such rules or even that such rules can be formulated. Is the reader aware, for example, why he says "call up the grocer" but does not say "call up her", preferring rather "call her up"? Similar to the widespread facility in language there is widespread facility in understanding visual messages. A "primitive" tribe produces sculptures and graphics even when its members are illiterate in terms of language. There may be a great human potential for iconic communication, following rules that no one has yet stated.

All normal human beings act on the basis of visual information. Even very young children find their way about, look at pictures in story books, and are entranced with movies and TV. The set of rules used for processing visual information, however, is unknown. We would be in a much more favorable position to generate iconic messages, now that generation is possible, if we understood how human beings interpret visual information. Pictures are intelligible to human beings from widely different cultural backgrounds, as the mass audience for TV attests.

Is it possible that linguistics and iconics are fundamentally the same? Could the basic notions of linguistics aid in understanding iconic communication? We will now explain why we believe the answers to these questions are essentially negative.

The field of linguistics is conveniently divided into three parts: syntax, the core subsystem of rules that tells how units (words, phonemes) are strung together; phonology, the physical form that phonemes take; and semantics, the interpretive subsystem whereby meanings are assigned according to the cultural milieu of the speaker. A sentence such as "green ideas sleep furiously" illustrates the relative contributions of syntax, phonology, and semantics. The sentence is syntactically well formed, an adjective precedes a noun, and the noun phrase is followed by a predicate made up of a verb plus modifier. It could be rendered intelligibly by different speakers. That is, if one speaker said "idears' instead of "ideas' the message would still be correctly processed by most speakers of American English even though its phonology varied. The sentence is semantically anomalous, however; it has no meaning. If the words were reordered "furiously green sleep ideas' so the syntactic content also is removed, the sentence would be called "random." It could still be pronounced, but it now violates conventions of syntax as well as semantics.

Suppose we try to transfer these linguistic notions to the analysis of sequences of pictures, like sequences that comprise a motion picture or the understanding of iconic communications more generally. The first question is: For iconics what is the analog of language? Language is the corpus of utterances for which the system of rules (linguistics) has been developed. For iconics, what is the body of data the science pertains to? A picture or other combination of visual signs seems to be the answer. But strings of pictures by themselves conveying messages, having meanings, without auditory accompaniments are rare. The only examples of soundless (captionless) pictures seem to be pantomimes or certain cartoon sequences. On the other hand, there are many instances of iconic images linked to verbal messages. Ordinary movies and television are the best examples. Iconic messages, then, rarely stand alone without accompanying language.

A second question is: What are the building blocks for iconics? Most visual images seen today are not generated from some kind of primitive visual forms but rather by stringing together photographic images of objects and events in the natural world. The TV producer goes to the desert to stage a desert scene, or takes his camera crew to the places where riots are occurring. (The analog for the author writing a book would be to search out in the library particular chapters, paragraphs, or sentences that he could string together to form a story.) How different it is to conceive of generating small parts of visual images and linking them together as the author does when he makes a sentence by taking individual words, perhaps even inventing words and arranging them in a sequence to convey his message. This is the possibility now at hand with computer-generated visual images. What may be created is limited only by the author's imagination. There is no need to record only visual forms associated with natural objects in the real world. However, the basic elements to use for conveying information to the visual sense have not been specified.

Other questions need to be considered: 1) What are the rules for combining the primitive elements of iconic communication, assuming they exist and can be defined? 2) What is the human potential for processing iconic messages? 3) What kinds of concepts can be conveyed using iconic messages alone or in combination with verbal messages? Obviously many more questions can be asked.

It seems to us (although we may be mistaken) that attempts to develop an analogy between iconics and linguistics are not very helpful in answering basic questions in iconics. A number of persons have written loosely about "visual literacy" or "picture syntax" but have not faced up to the issues these terms imply. We have not found, for instance, principles for combining images that are analogous to syntax, the principles for stringing words together. In fact, the even more fundamental question raised above--what are the basic elements in iconics that are analogous to words--is puzzling. What is the "unit" of an image? Is it a single frame in a length of movie film, or some cognitive abstraction that might be labeled "John running," or some small component of a picture like a dot or a line? Linguistics deals with morphemes or phonemes. What are the comparable units of analysis in iconics?

Another source of confusion in iconics is the dependence, earlier mentioned, of iconic messages upon linguistic messages. As earlier noted, "pure" iconic messages like pantomimes are rare. Iconic communications are usually linked to verbal communications, pictures and sounds on TV, pictures in textbooks, or narrations to accompany computer-generated films, so the message has independent contributions from the iconic and linguistic components plus some component due to their interaction. With this kind of linkage, part of the meaning of a movie film is communicated by the sound track but either the film footage alone or the sound track alone convey much less meaning.

The interaction between linguistic and iconic messages can be illustrated by considering further examples. A diagram of an electric circuit in an engineering text displays some meanings easily conveyed by the text, but it also communicates easily other meanings that are expressed by language only with great difficulty. On reading that a circuit has five nodes, A through E, interconnected AB, AC, AE, BD,and CD, one has all the information necessary to draw the circuit's configuration. Yet without the drawing, the information is hard to hold in mind and process. Strictly speaking the drawing is completely equivalent to the verbal description. The drawing adds no new semantic content to the message at its source, but it does make it easier for most receivers to recover the message. Most people find such verbal descriptions without a diagram almost unintelligible.

In addition iconic components can add semantic content that is not redundant with any verbal message because language is poor at encoding unambiguously certain ideas and concepts.

How could one describe in words the patterns of light and shade produced by a breeze on a sunlit birch tree? For one thing, the qualities of light and color, as perceived, depend on the surroundings. A yellow of a particular wavelength can appear "light" or "dark", or even "green", with various backgrounds. For encoding this kind of information verbal schemes are impoverished, yet even a young child can easily observe the tree.

The science of linguistics does not appear to offer much direct aid for the analysis of iconic communication. For us, what iconic messages seem to offer and what a science of iconics should deal with are properties that verbal messages do not possesS: spatial arrangements and motion. Many phenomena of importance to human beings in the natural world involve spatial deployment of objects or persons and successive rearrangements of these through time. Concepts involving space and motion are only conveyed clumsily, if at all, using a verbal or symbolic encoding. We have already taken the example of a 5-node circuit. For another example consider the design of such a simple thing as a foot bridge. To specify this using only sentences and no diagrams or pictures, would be very difficult. Or to specify by only verbal means the successive positions of a ball as it rolls down an inclined plane would be equally difficult. What is needed, then, is not a science of iconics that apes that of linguistics but an independent set of principles geared to the two basic attributes of iconic messages, spatial arrangements, and motion. Elsewhere (Chapter VII) we have attempted to distill from our own experience and from the recorded experience of others, information useful in framing visual messages where space and motion are involved.

We end this chapter by pointing to some larger problems that a science of iconics should eventually face. (1) Iconics must deal with innate human capacities to abstract and process complicated visual information. Young children can recognize complicated pictures after long periods of time. How is this done? How long does such retention persist? (2) Iconics should be concerned with and try to define universals. What kinds of iconic communication are readily understood by most human beings? What effect does culture have on perception of spatial and moving arrangements? (3) A viewer can interpret pictures he has not seen before. How different from previous experience can iconic messages be? (4) Individual differences are likely in the ability to use or to generate iconic messages. Could human beings be trained to process more or different iconic information? People learn to read, by which we mean they learn to find meaning in arbitrary grapheme cues. Could people learn a new kind of "reading" where the elements were defined in terms of spatial or dynamic properties? In other words, could people learn to use an "alphabet" with symbols not sequentially presented and not static? (5) How could a science of iconics aid education and learning? How can the properties of motion and spatial arrangement be manipulated to produce visual models, unlike any visual phenomena occurring in nature, to exemplify concepts?

IV. ICONICS AND EDUCATION

Education as practiced today depends very little on iconic information. The printed word is symbolic, and the traditional ways of communicating in education are symbolic even where basic concepts may be strongly geometrical. Systems of equations or symbolic models dominate the sciences and engineering, even though the concepts to be communicated often involve relative motion, spatial displacement, and the like. It seems more sensible to present in an iconic mode those concepts having a structure that might be represented by spatial arrangements or motion. Thus, to show how sine waves of different periods may be combined to produce a square wave is easily explained in an iconic mode. Means for generating images to explain many important ideas in mathematics, physics, and engineering are now at hand. The technological capability for producing iconic messages for use in education, in fact, far outstrips the demand for such messages. (For an up-to-date review of computer animation resources and an extensive bibliography, see WEINER 1971).

Why is there an avoidance of iconic messages in education? It is partly attributable to resistance to change--teachers fluent in mathematics are not apt to desert the library in favor of the production studio. But partly the problem resides in our ignorance about how to form iconic expressions. What topics in education are suitable for an iconic metaphor? And having decided the metaphor is appropriate, how do we form and utilize it?

Present uses of iconic messages commonly rely on a basic isomorphism between the iconic model and the physical reality it represents. A slide of the Mona Lisa bears a very strong pictorial resemblance to the actual painting. What about iconic models where the isomorphism is not strong, where it is even weak or absent? A motion picture of computer-generated waveforms is in some sense more isomorphic to the concept of decomposition into harmonic components than would be pictures of actual waves because attention can be directed to the abstract properties of waves in general rather than to incidental variations and irrelevant detail that accompany particular physical occurrences of waves. A film showing the solar system with planets moving about the sun may look very much like what a viewer stationed outside the solar system could see if he waited long enough. On two attributes, however, (like the film of waveforms) the model of the solar system departs from the reality it is depicting. It is scaled in both time and space to facilitate perception. The point is that most iconic messages developed up to the present time have been isomorphic in a very fundamental sense with the phenomena they represent. Part of our concern with problems in iconic communication arose from considering problems with a high degree of isomorphism, like the one just cited concerning waves.

But there is another concern: How to depict concepts visually in the absence of strong isomorphism. A different order of problem is raised by issues we faced in the small film "Dynamic Symbols," later to be described in more detail. In this film we wanted to convey the notions of flow in an electric circuit, of the difference between active and passive elements (some elements like batteries are the sources of electric flow while others, like resistors, rely on other sources to cause a current), and of how the quantity of flow divides when more than one path is available. There is no simple obvious way to represent these notions visually in ways analogous to the solar system example. In the solar system model, as earlier remarked, the elements are vastly reduced in size and the rate of movement is increased, but the spatial relationships and the motion itself, particularly in terms of what moves, are preserved intact. In the physical electric circuit containing a battery and some resistors, the human viewer cannot directly observe any motion nor is there any visible external characteristic of the elements that would obviously relate their appearance to their function. A young child, for example, can see that a battery and a resistor differ in their physical appearance but this is quite unrelated to their electrical properties. That a battery generates flow and has a different property than a resistor, is not apparent to the child because current and voltage are not naturally visible. Instead these physical "observables' must be translated into observable form by meters in which a mechanical pointer moves in proportion to the magnitude of the current, or, as in the case of modern digital voltmeters, a numerical value is displayed--but this is an arbitrary choice by convention. It is not evident that mapping onto a numerical scale is the best way of showing these relations iconically. A better scheme may be to represent the measure of the quantity by a physical length rather than by a number. Several such lengths may be "added" geometrically to show the additive composition of several physical currents. (See HUGGINS 1968 for a discussion of a "lollipop" meter symbol that is quite effective.).

The spatial relationships among the elements are important in some cases (resistors in series or parallel), so this iconic attribute can be the same in the model as in the real world, but some rather arbitrary scheme for showing the electric flow is required to represent a circuit iconically. The motion in the film of the solar system was of the same type and direction as the planetary motion in the solar system itself, just enormously speeded up in time so the observer could see a year's change in a minute or so. However, planetary motion is explained since Newton by gravitational forces that express the tendency of two separate masses to accelerate toward one another. Although the accelerated motion can be shown iconically, there is no direct way to show the gravitational force itself. Some arbitrary convention like an arrow whose length and direction correspond to the magnitude and direction of the force must be introduced to represent the force. Similarly, in the electric circuit there is no obvious way to depict voltage. The voltage at the source is not reflected in any obvious way by the source's appearance as the mass of a planet is reflected in its appearance. What this dilemma leads to is the need for an arbitrary iconic convention to display voltage. There is no direct means, based on a spatial relationship or motion (the two fundamental characteristics of an iconic message) to model a visual presentation of a circuit upon the natural appearance of the real-world circuit. Some artificial or arbitrary convention is required to make use of these two fundamental iconic properties.

Now we pose the fundamental problem of iconics: How to use the visual abilities of human beings already highly developed through lifelong processing of natural iconic images to design and employ a new range of iconic images and symbols. Most of the graphical schemes, such as circuit diagrams commonly used today, have been developed for use on the printed page or paper. As such they are static and closely connected with the accompanying text. It is not surprising that the conventions used in constructing such diagrams echo the restrictions implicit in the mathematical or verbal descriptions of the system being represented. For instance, the idea of a force field (such as that due to gravity around the sun) is made mathematically concrete by focusing attention on the magnitude and direction of the force at a typical point in space. Then, the force at this point may be represented pictorially by an arrow whose length describes the magnitude of the force and whose direction describes its direction. This convention is so familiar and widely used that its inadequacies are seldom recognized. For one, the essential property of the gravitational field is its continuous pervasiveness throughout all space--the field exists everywhere, not just at an isolated point. The attention to a single point is permissible only because one has already invoked the analytical assumptions and mathematical framework of linear decomposition of the whole into a collection of infinitesimal parts. The essential property of the field is that this force acts simultaneously at all points in space. This property is very poorly conveyed by showing force arrows. Of course, one may use many arrows simultaneously to show the forces at a sampling of different points throughout the region of interest, but this bristling porcupine of a display is an even more atrocious portrayal of the smooth continuous nature of the field as a whole.

As an alternative to the use of arrow "vectors" to represent a force field, Faraday introduced flux lines of flow (or motion) which describe the trajectories along which elementary weightless particles might be visualized as moving under the influence of the field. While superior to the bristling porcupine representation, these field lines are likewise deficient as a scheme for iconic representation of a field, particularly if the field is nonconservative and time varying. For instance, in this scheme, the intensity of the field is conveyed by the spacing between the adjacent streamlines--the closer they are, the greater the intensity of the field (much like the iso-elevation lines on a topographical map). Suppose we wish to show the gravitational field and its relative intensity at any point above the surface in the equatorial plane of the earth. The intensity is known to vary inversely as the square of the distance to the center of the earth. Hence the radial flow lines should have a spacing at any distance R which is proportional to $1/R^2$. But this is impossible. (Continuous lines having the requisite spacing in a plane are possible only if the intensity varies as $1/R$, but the inverse square relationship cannot be satisfied.) Hence, the familiar diagram found in most physics books that purports to show the field intensity in a plane violates quantitatively the convention for intensity. Furthermore, if the field is changing in time, new lines must appear discontinuously from nowhere while others vanish into nothingness abruptly, and spurious implications of motion of the field lines can be created, all of which convey false or erroneous information to the viewer. It seems to us that an iconic representation having motion and spatial perspective need not take the same form as the traditional static diagram used in books. The representation used should be especially devised to suit the medium. Basic studies of iconic symbols are badly needed to suggest how such representation should be carried out.

A whole new realm of human information processing may lie ready to be discovered if a new notation using dynamic symbols can be devised. In other words, we are suggesting a new set of "iconic" symbols deployed in a 2- or 3-space (rather than in a linear string) and where symbols move about and gain part of their meaning from their motion and spatial relationships.

The possibilities here are manifold. A very exciting one is the use of an ecologically valid representation--the human face--to encode information (CHERNOFF 1971). Human beings are trained from birth to attend to minute details of human faces and to read the expression upon them (see eg GOLDSTEIN 1971; 1972). This "pre-training" can be called into service to process other kinds of information.

Using up to 17 parameters to control shape of the head, location and shape of the eyebrows, curvature and width of the mouth, orientation of the eyes, etc., one can construct a computer program that will draw a caricature of the human face and thus encode a vast amount of information (see Figure IV-1). Although human beings might find it tedious to compare and remember vectors of numbers with 17 elements, they seem to be marvelously adept at responding to faces corresponding to these vectors. Such schemes for presenting information are just coming under study. Working under the direction of W. H. Huggins, Robert Jacob produced the faces shown in Fig. IV-1. with the ultimate objective of using these methods to present in quickly perceived form the health indicators of patients in an intensive-care hospital ward.

Figure IV-1. Chernoff Faces.

V. ICONICS AND PSYCHOLOGY

Psychology has enormously expanded the range of its research since 1950. Motivation, for example, is no longer restricted entirely to abrasive events like the deprivation of food, of water, of sex, or the sensation of pain. Instead, motivation is now seen to be shaped around positive goals, things like the need to play, the need to manipulate, and most important for us, the need to be stimulated, the need to perceive and to perceive clearly. Whereas learning used to be viewed as a phenomenon that could be diminished or encumbered by such things as massed trials, predictable reinforcement, reinforcement delays, or inappropriate reinforcement, happily now psychologists are focusing on what helps learning or aids the learner. Imagery or visual elaboration is one such force which enhances learning. Imagery is the present topic of much vigorous psychological research. In this section we will sketch in our notions of how imagery aids perception and of what imagery consists. Later we will review some psychological research on imagery that relates to iconic communication.

Study of the relation between visual imagery and cognition is currently enjoying a revival among American psychologists. Many of them support Arnheim's (1969) thesis that visual imagery plays a central role in thinking. Bugelski (1970) writes (p 1011) "My current leaning is toward the belief that few of us, if any, actually think in abstract terms when we are doing our everyday routine thinking. I rather suspect, with Mowrer (1960) that we think with our gut and rather individual imagery and that our idiosyncratic reactions are responsible for the considerable lack of communications in conversations that relate to serious social problems. Words have a way of arousing images, and if the images are not the same, communication fails."

The relation between symbol and picture has been described from a developmental point of view by Jerome Bruner (1966), who suggests that acquisition and understanding of information may proceed through three stages illustrated by of Figure V-1 diagram.

In the life course of a human being, the mind seems to develop along these three levels. There is evidence of an innate tendency forcing man up this inverted pyramid to symbolize his experiences. By giving names to his perceptual and enactive experiences, man is able to abstract certain aspects of these experiences in a form that may be communicated and recorded. By so doing he stabilizes and socializes his private perceptions.

Following Bruner, the symbolic mode of communication is shown at the "highest" level, resting upon the iconic and enactive levels for definition and ultimate meaning.

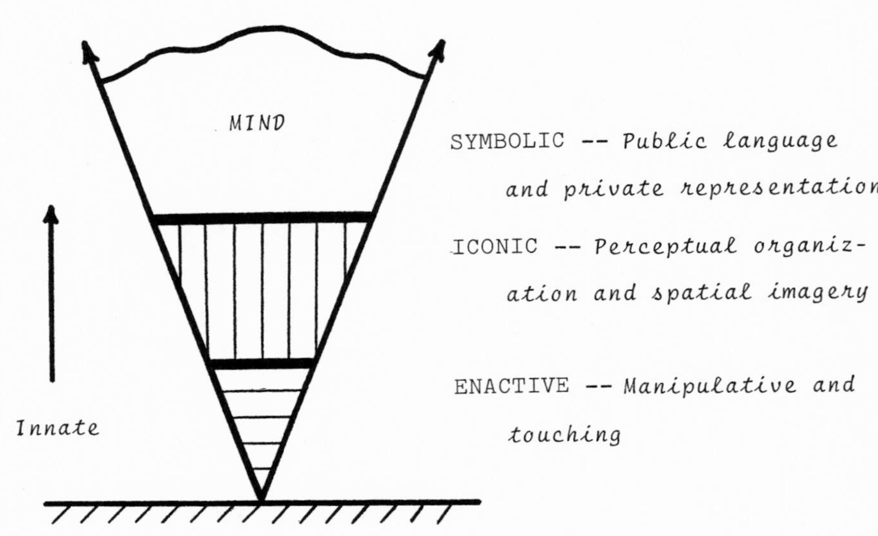

Figure V-1. Bruner's Three Modes of Communication

In the life course of a human being, the mind seems to develop along these three levels. There is evidence of an innate tendency forcing man up this inverted pyramid to symbolize his experiences. By giving names to his perceptual and enactive experiences, man is able to abstract certain aspects of these experiences in a form that may be communicated and recorded. By so doing he stabilizes and socializes his private perceptions.

The drive to symbolize carries with it some puzzling and fascinating implications. Research on vision suggests that there is a short-term storage of the visual image in its full photographic detail and that information is almost at once transformed in some way (see NEISSER 1967, Chapters 1 and 2). It is as though the details of the picture are encoded into some more efficient form permitting internal classification and subsequent processing. For most persons, this iconic storage is short-lived (of the order of a few tenths of a second), but for some individuals with eidetic imagery, the photographic-like image can be retained for long periods of time and examined later for details not originally perceived.

If imagery is important to human thought, why has the effective employment of visual images eluded computer scientists? Practitioners of computer science, like those of many other disciplines, seem to be able to function entirely at the symbolic level with no need to communicate at the iconic or enactive levels of human experience. Their world is apparently a syntactical structure of symbol strings. This has had unfortunate consequences, for it has led computer-graphics as a field to attend to the hardware and nonhuman problems rather than to problems in iconic communication. The inattention of computer scientists generally to problems in human communication was one of the major reasons for our production of this book.

The issues raised by Bruner are crucial to education. As television has pushed students increasingly toward iconic modes of communication, classroom instruction in many disciplines, paradoxically, has become increasingly mathematical, symbolic, and abstract. Computer-aided instruction, when present, usually adds to this buzzing confusion of symbols. Is it possible that part of present-day students' call for "relevance" is really a cry for help in assigning some meaning to the sea of undefined symbols that engulfs them? Is "relevance" to be interpreted in a cognitive as well as social context?

Perhaps when he achieves the difficult task of symbolizing, man prefers to ignore the steps up the enactive and iconic ladder that he had to climb to endow his own symbolic constructions with meaning. The educator may face a particularly serious hazard because having learned and relearned his material, he may completely suppress modes of thought he used to achieve his present state of expertise. He may underestimate the necessity of providing sufficient enactive and iconic experience for new learners. If the learner has a well-defined symbolic system matching that of the teacher, he may be strong enough to by-pass the first two stages and communicate purely at the symbolic level. But the learner then may not possess the imagery to fall back upon when his symbolic transformations later fail to solve a problem. Or the learner may adopt a preliminary "more basic" conceptual strategy, an iconic one, before he can grasp the intuitive meaning of a symbolic representation. For many persons, it may be impossible, inefficient, or even wasteful to rely completely on a symbolic mode of communication. Also, who knows what new implications and structures for problem solving might come from an appropriate iconic translation?

Man has the ability both to create speech and to listen, and the rate at which speech may be produced is within the same order of magnitude as the rate at which it can be perceived. Now, constrast this with vision. Man's eyes can take in information at an enormously greater rate than his ears. The excess ability to acquire visual information may be one cause for "all input and no output." People generally do not make visual symbols easily and their self-consciousness in such efforts as they do make perhaps stems from the fact that their mental imagery remains private, unseen, and unidentified with the self.

A few further words are needed about the development of "imaging ability." Bruner's formulation of iconic development has not been studied much empirically. Recent suggestions by

Rohwer (1970) point to a continuing iconic stage, paralleling the symbolic stage. However this may be, we need to know more about human processing of iconic data.

Anthropologists have had a lively interest in how pictorial images are interpreted by persons of non-Western cultures (eg see HEIDER 1971). Following Hudson's (1960) invention of a test to assess ability to perceive a third dimension in 2-dimensional pictures, many cross-cultural studies have appeared relating the recognition of various depth perception cues and the amount of respondents' education to performance.

This area of research has serious, perhaps insurmountable, methodological problems. For one thing, it is virtually impossible to design a test situation that is equally "fair" or comprehensible. But the main stumbling block is that internal perceptual events can be "recognized" by a tester only when the testee reports them. Deregowski (1968) shows that "2-D perceivers' as identified by Hudson's test can readily construct 3-D models when a construction task is furnished. A "2-D perceiver" may process cues and act upon them without being able to call these into conscious awareness. The same drawbacks attach to using the lexicon as evidence of what a culture can perceive. Berry (cited by WOBER 1966) points out that certain African languages lack words for identifying and analyzing visual designs. The Temme tongue, for instance, is without words for several geometrical shapes labeled in Western language. But lack of words is no reliable clue to perceptual activity or ability as is shown by the Dani (HEIDER 1971). Their language is bare of color names but they can easily learn to label and distinguish among colors when colors not present naturally are introduced into the environment and made "relevant."

Cross-cultural studies of imaging may turn out to be unproductive for much the same reasons that earlier studies of the visual illusions have yielded remarkably little information. Special cases and counter-examples are productive if an elaborate conceptual scheme already exists. This is, sadly, not the case in iconics.

Ten years ago there would have been little to say about the relation between iconics and psychology. Fortunately for us, psychologists have been working on imagery at the same time that our concern has centered around visual images produced by computer-based techniques for making movie film. No actual research yet links these two independent lines of work, but they are of great significance for one another. This chapter has had the purpose of pointing up the mutual relations of these two research trends.

Psychologists see imagery as relating to thinking, learning, and problem-solving (eg HOTTENLOCHER 1968). The filmmaker interested in producing films for instructional use would like to understand exactly how visual imagery aids learning or retention. He can now look to psychology for some help with these questions. Film producers, on the other hand, have the technological means psychologists lack to support empirical research. Psychologists need artificial images for use in experimentation that until now were too difficult to produce. Hopefully this bibliography will bring psychologists and computer technologists together by documenting their mutual concerns.

VI. RESEARCH ON IMAGERY

We first summarize some of the recent psychological literature concerned with imagery from the viewpoint of iconic communication. We will pay little attention to how this research affects psychological theory or experiments generally, and we will reinterpret the research when necessary to emphasize its relevance for iconics.

Verbal learning theory notices that particular verbal stimuli can come (by learning) to elicit particular verbal responses. It is presumed that stimulus and response are linked (associated) by some process occurring within the organism. Some theorists, like Skinner, have eschewed any consideration of this internal process; others have hypothesized certain neurophysiological processes intervening. Still others have tried to invent information-processing models without trying to specify the physiological process underlying. Whatever the linkage, many workers have implicitly assumed that mediating processes are verbal, that whatever is activated inside the organism is encoded using verbal parameters. Until recently almost no mention has been made of possible nonverbal or "perceptual imagery" mediating processes (DEESE 1965).

Bugelski (1970) has recently called attention to the possible role of imagery in cognition. He reviews research on nonverbal mediators. A very brief overview of some of Bugelski's main points will serve to link the field of cognitive psychology as a whole with issues pertinent for iconics.

In word-association studies subjects are usually asked to give "the first word that comes to mind" after hearing a stimulus word. For example, if the word "table" is spoken by the experimenter the subject is asked to respond quickly with a word. With this instructional set it is no suprise that the subject gives a verbal response. Bugelski points to the biasing of the response caused by such instructions. To avoid this, Bugelski conducted an experiment in which he asked college students to write down "the very first thing they thought of" when they heard some stimulus words. It turned out that hardly any of the first things they thought of were other words--only 15 of over 1800 responses were words. When subjects wrote descriptions of what they thought of, some of the descriptions portrayed vivid imagery and were highly imaginative. To the word "communism" one subject imaged "a red velvet wall with a large yellow hammer and sickle." Perhaps even more significant, there was much greater heterogeneity among subjects' responses when the task was presented using the "thing" instructions compared to responses following "first word" instructions.

Bugelski's results suggest that visual images may underlie thought processes, but this can be easily obscured by the rather incidental conditions of an experiment. If the role of imagery is considerable, as suggested by Bugelski's work, the next question is what is involved in "imaging." How is imaging related to perception and thinking?

A central question in psychology is how to arrange or encode stimuli so that they will be optimal for learning. To answer this question we need to know the functional significance of nonverbal and verbal processes in associative meaning, mediation, and memory (see PAIVIO 1970). Everyday experiences makes the acceptance of mental images compelling.

Problem-solving performance (see HUTTENLOCHER 1968) also testifies to the importance of forming mental images. (For instance Shepard 1966 p 203) says "if I am now asked the number of windows in my house, I find that I must picture the house, as viewed from different sides, or from within different rooms and then count the windows presented in these various mental images."

As Paivio emphasizes, an eliciting question and the behavioral expression of recall may be entirely verbal but the mediation mechanism need not be. Paivio also points out that to infer images as mediators between stimulus and response is logically no different than inferring implicit verbal processes--both are constructs not available to direct observation.

An important assumption underlying iconic communication generally is that visual images of concrete events and objects are particularly vivid and therefore are well remembered. To this assumption, generally voiced explicitly or implicitly by psychologists who see imagery as important for cognition, we add the "explanation" of vividness. Pictorial representation in space and motion add, in effect, two more dimensions for coding information that verbal mediators lack, without interfering with or detracting from whatever verbal coding dimensions are in use.

In the psychological literature to date there has been much attention directed toward pictorial representation with little attention to what "pictorial" means. Paivio (1970) analyzes the pictorial representation effect as a "conceptual peg"--high-imagery stimuli function as efficient stimulus pegs from which associates can be hung. He feels (p 388) that this hypothesis has been repeatedly confirmed. Actually it is not clear what Paivio has in mind for an "efficient stimulus peg."

Bower (1970) sees two possible explanations for imagery effects, a differentation type and an association type. His differentiation type holds that encoding by imagery leads to a more distinctive functional stimulus. This seems to be a clearer statement of the peg hypothesis. His second explanation--the association type--holds that an imagery association requires the subject to find a relation between two items. It could have to do with the linking of two semantic concepts. He presents data favoring the association type explanation.

We believe that, like most alternative explanations, probably both play a role and the influence of each factor depends on the particular situation. Rohwer's (1970) point of view seems consistent with a dual explanation.

Rohwer studied elaboration strategies in relation to learning. For example, when pairs of words are to be learned in a paired-associate learning task, subjects can be asked to "elaborate" on them by imaging some combination of the two objects. If the task is to learn "plate" in response to "bus," (1) the subject might try to visualize a plate and a bus simultaneously in his mind, or (2) he might image a plate on top of a bus, or (3) he might image a bus out of control crossing home plate on a baseball diamond. These images were chosen to exemplify (1) a passive depicting of the two objects, (2) use of spatial ordering to link the two objects, (3) use of episodic (dynamic) events to associate the objects. Clearly (2) and (3) are making some added use of visual properties of images that increase the vividness of the relationship between the two words that are to be linked.

In (1) the strategy is merely to image two objects without using their spatial relationships as a cue for associating them. Visual encoding--like strategy (2) based on spatial relationships--exploits an attribute peculiar to the visual mode. It introduces, in effect, another dimension into the coding scheme. The subject invents an image with spatial arrangement of the objects--"on top," "on either side of a road," "hidden behind," and the like--and uses this relationship as a cue. Work by us (ENTWISLE 1973), by Haber (1969B), and Kagan (1970) suggests that the spatial dimension is a particularly powerful one in terms of human data-processing capabilitiesS. Animals up the phylogenetic tree become more and more capable of using spatial cues and remembering. Spatial relationships, when called into service, offer a potentially rich method for encoding other relationships.

Visual encoding, like strategy (3) based on episodic cues, probably always includes use of spatial relationships. The bus is visualized in some 3-space in relation to home plate, but strategy (3) adds more. The property of motion involves changes of spatial relationships, a dynamic element in other words. "Episodic coding," a term used by psychologists, means a coding in terms of dynamic spatial relationships. If spatial relationships are effective parameters to use in coding information, then dynamic spatial relationships should be even more powerful aids to association than static spatial relationships as long as data-processing capabilities were not overtaxed.

Rohwer does not link his "spatial-relational" and "episodic-thematic" ideas about elaboration either to Bower's explanations for imagery effects or to our ideas about the properties of visual stimuli. However these three approaches are highly compatible. An "episodic-thematic" elaboration introduces some new dimensions by which to associate objects--a bus running over home plate involves both objects in an action that can be imaged. The image in this case "tells a story," creating an association. This effect is in addition to any possible advantage obtained by mentally visualizing the two objects. For many such "episodic-thematic" elaborations, like this one, motion of objects, which we see as a very important dimension of visual stimuli, is also involved.

To date, as far as we know, visual elaboration has been explored only in terms of paired associates--associating one word with another so that upon presentation of the first, the second will be produced. (The use of paired-associates in learning experiments comes about because of need for experimental control.) It seems likely, however, if imagery strategies confer benefits in learning pairs of words, such strategies would be considerably more beneficial for tasks of greater complexity, like learning of some physical principle or learning of historical sequences. The physical principle of the fulcrum, for instance, offers opportunities for rich imagery that might aid comprehension as well as retention. The learner may visualize one small child sitting on a see-saw with his parent seated on the other side practically on the hinge.

Thus far, aids to visual elaboration have been limited to still pictures--no moving pictures have been used. For certain kinds of learning, like the fulcrum principle mentioned above, a dynamic elaboration may be essential for the concept to be communicated. For simpler cognitive tasks, like that of associating two "unrelated" words such as "bus" and "plate", motion would provide vivid elaboration. Seeing a film of a bus careening wildly through a baseball field and crossing home plate might produce such startling elaboration that the two words would be forever associated. In any case, the potential for dynamic elaboration needs to be explored.

VII. APPLICATION OF ICONICS.

Computer-Generated Film.

The use of computers to produce animated film began about a decade ago. A survey of its development, with a desciption of the various programming systems and techniques that have been used, and a guide to current activities (together with an extensive bibliography of 129 references and of more than 80 films that have been produced by various workers) has recently been published by Weiner (1971). Accordingly, we mention here only those aspects that are particularly relevant to iconic communication or that are not reported by Weiner.

Most of the early computer animated movies were done by writing appropriate computer-graphic commands in FORTRAN. Subsequent efforts involved developing new programming languages specifically tailored to simplify the making of movies. A pioneering effort was Knowlton's BEFLIX which contained many commands, like ZOOM, to perform the kinds of operations and transformations needed to simulate a camera. Another movie language called PMACRO was developed by Huggins to make several computer-animated films that have been distributed by the National Committee on Electrical Engineering Films. All of the languages, however, require the specification of the graphical images by punching standard IBM cards in accord with symbolic instructions used to create the various computer programs needed. Hence, although the end product was an iconic film, the specification was purely symbolic. A major forward step was taken by Baecker(1969A, 1969B), who developed the GENESYS system whereby an animator can specify on a screen the images to be moved about and the schedule for motion. In this on-line system images are drawn by the animator and require no symbolic programming.

More elaborate off-line methods, based on list processing languages and elaborate data structures, were devised by Anderson and Weiner (1968) and Knowlton (1964, 1965). They culminate in the filming of images displayed on a graphic terminal. Talbot and his associates (1971) have tried to fuse the on-line interactive approaches with the more powerful off-line remote approach. Using a specialized hierarchical language, the user prepares a "rough draft" of his movie in a "picture definition mode" and then enters a "transmission mode" for final movie production.

Less elaborate off-line procedures currently available include one developed at Johns Hopkins (HOFFMANN 1972) that uses a FORTRAN-based language M*O*G*U*L with an IBM 7094 (or more powerful) computer to generate data tapes. The data tapes can be processed at one of several installations having a STROMBERG-CARLSON 4020, and the film made from the data tape returned by mail. This last method is relatively slow and tedious but could be widely used since the user does not require specialized equipment. The M*O*G*U*L package includes a simulation routine which will produce, at very little cost, rough graphic output on a high-speed line printer. Such printed output gives the animator rough feedback prior to production of a complete film.

Efficient production of movies depends on suitable programming languages. That is, one must produce a series of frames that differ from one another only slightly and yet in an extremely precise way. A language like M*O*G*U*L makes it possible to issue instructions so that whole series of frames result from a single statement made by a programmer. It is possible, for example, with a single instruction to draw a geometric figure like a square at a desired location in a 1000 X 1000 grid space. This square can them be moved at a desired rate of speed so that it will end at a new location specified by the programmer. This easy process must be compared to the costly process of hand animation where successive drawings must be produced in large numbers to achieve the finished product of a square moving across the screen. Other applications that are more complicated--addition of complex wave forms for instance--hold special importance for technical education. These are intrinsically no more difficult to program than other simple figures. The enormous computational facility of the computer allows exact representations to be derived from mathematically expressed functions.

Producing film, as already made clear, involves the writing and running of computer programs, but initially a film must be carefully worked out on paper by creating a story-board. Then the desired sequences are translated into an appropriate computer language (KNOWLTON 1964, SARNO 1968, HUGGINS 1968, HOFFMANN 1972). As mentioned above, with suitable languages it is easy to specify how figures are to move around the screen. The most difficult part of the process--the initial conception of the film and its translation to graphic images on a story-board--is the most neglected. Although the technology for producing films has improved tremendously over the past decade, there has been no corresponding progress in the thought-to-story-board translation. This neglect is one sign of the need for a science of iconics.

The technical advantages of computer-animated films have been well discussed elsewhere (KNOWLTON 1965) and so will be reviewed only briefly. Animation produced in this way can be much less costly than traditional animation (overall costs, exclusive of the programmers time, for a polished final product have run at about $300 per minute of final film).

Also one person can do a complete motion picture, from conception of the idea through production of the final version. The production of elaborate visual sequences is economically feasible provided the final product is recorded on film (or video-tape) for low-cost duplication and distribution to many viewers. Costs, in other words, must be interpreted in terms of overall usefulness.

At present many computer systems exist with visual displays--thus one might think of individual tutoring of students with each student at a console with his own visual-display unit. For most schools, this is at present much too expensive to consider. It is cumbersome because equipment cannot be moved around, and such elaborate systems require well-trained personnel to oversee their use. The computer's versatility however, when set to the task of film production, yields a product that is easily transportable, that is relatively cheap, and that requires little in the way of technical competence to use. Although computer-graphic terminals would be nice to have at every school, these elaborate (and costly) facilities are by no means essential because they can be replaced by the computer generated film or video tape.

For explaining some concepts and abstractions in the sciences and engineering, computer-generated film has advantages over any other medium. Such films can show aspects of physical events that can be computed but never directly observed. For instance, Loomis simulated the motion of the basilar membrane of the inner ear and made a computer-generated movie showing the vibration of this membrane in response to various sounds. This vibration could never be observed in toto. Yet, by using fundamental measurements made on the inner ear by von Bekesy (for which he received the Nobel prize), Loomis was able to reveal an aspect of reality that is beyond direct observation. Similarly, one may compute, and thus display, the instantaneous temperature and pressure at every point inside of a slab of armor-plate when an explosive charge is detonated on its surface. Until now events like these could be portrayed only crudely, and inaccurately if at all, and at prohibitive cost by making studio films of demonstrations using elaborate special equipment.

Computer-generated films have advantages in terms of evaluation studies (later we will describe some field tests of such films that we have conducted) because they make it feasible to study alternate schemes for displaying concepts. They allow one to develop at low cost a wide range of different visual materials. These test films can be tried out with students and revised easily and quickly. This makes evaluation of educational movies in the field much more feasible than formerly.

Our research has aimed at concentrating on the strengths and unique aspects of computer-animation, especially the ability to present moving signs that evolve. A new medium should tackle communication problems it can solve differently or better than pre-existing media. To have a film of an instructor lecturing makes little use of the unique qualities or capabilities of film beyond simple replacement of the lecturer. Movement, in particular, is a property that symbols printed or written have never before possessed but with which computer animation can now endow them. Potentially a new dimension is added to the kind of information symbols can convey. For communicating scientific and engineering concepts, this dimension may offer much, since many of these concepts concern structural relationships among things and how the relationships change.

Our basic notion is that a new medium, the moving iconic symbol, is now available and that its own special strengths need to be explored and developed. What is required is a breaking away from standard teaching techniques and an exploration of the possibilities offered by the new technology of computer-generated displays.

In making a computer-animated film, if one deliberately avoids the use of traditional words and mathematical symbols and attempts instead to portray all abstract ideas iconically, he quickly learns that "one word is worth a thousand pictures." He also soon discovers that many of the signs traditionally used in science and engineering are inadequate for conveying many familiar concepts without first introducing irrelevant details fraught with erroneous artifacts and implications. For instance, in a film requiring signs for representing various properties of electric circuits, we found it very difficult to indicate cause-effect relations. We finally used, for lack of anything better, an inelegant anthropomorphic symbol shaped like a human hand to change the value of the source signal on which other signals depend. Clearly, here is a fundamental notion for which no simple pictorial convention is available (see MICHOTTE 1963). There are many other similar needs.

Another unsolved problem, mentioned in an earlier chapter, is how to portray a continuum field, such as the electric potential around a set of electronic charges. The portrayal of a vector field using the familiar stream lines (or lines of force) leaves much to be desired because the direction of the lines is not easily shown, (eg arrow heads introduced along the lines created broken-line segments that violate the portrayal of smooth continuity of the field). Furthermore, when one attempts to superimpose two such fields, as in demonstrating the superposition of forward- and backward-traveling waves on a transmission line, a whole host of spurious effects result as field lines cross each other or vanish and reappear from nowhere and perform other atrocities. These difficulties arise even in showing simple, two-dimensional fields; traditional conventions are completely inadequate for portraying general vector fields in three dimensions. New ideas are badly needed for representational schemes that will be free of bothersome artifacts.

We believe that there is tremendous untapped potential in the use of iconic modes of communication to give fuller definition to the symbols dominating today's classroom. This belief has prompted us to prepare a self-instructing text to teach the major concepts of modern system theory by using the highly iconic notation of signal-flow graphs (HUGGINS and ENTWISLE 1968). Student response to this approach has been very enthusiastic. In another vein, the studies of Rohwer (1967) also point to the possible benefits from using nonverbal symbols. He shows that pictorial presentation of pairs of objects to elementary-school children leads to better association between the objects than presentation of pairs of words representing the objects.

What may be true is that an iconic stage in human ontogeny, largely ignored, has had an aborted development. Who knows what the potentialities may be? Young children, lower-class adults (people who are not "hooked" on reading), are those most addicted to TV--perhaps there is a vast starvation for meaningful communication that has never been met by standard media using printing.

Testing of a Specific Film: "Dynamic Symbols"

A major purpose of our research with computer-animated films has been to develop several movie presentations of scientific or engineering topics using a very simple dynamic notation. We have been chary of adopting standard symbolism such as that used in conventional circuit theory and have tried to invent a simpler, more easily generated symbolism that would have particular properties needed to imply in some natural sense the important ideas to be communicated.

For instance, the symbol for a resistor is a rectangle that has an inside region rather than the zig-zag line commonly used in the United States. By placing a meter symbol inside of this region, we hoped the viewer would get the idea that the meter measured flow through the resistor. Likewise, the battery (source) was represented by a diamond shape, which like the rectangle has an inside region that contains a meter symbol.

For the meter symbol, we used a small circle which is displaced from a reference line by a distance representative of the magnitude of the current. The advantage of this "lollipop" meter is that the displacement occurs in the same direction as the current flow and because of its extreme simplicity, the indication of the amount of current is shown with utmost visual clarity (unlike a conventional meter with its irrelevant scale and pointer). In fact, we believe this "lollipop" meter offers an iconically superior scheme for showing simultaneously the values of the many observables associated with an iconic representation of a complicated system.

An early experimental film made by Eugene Stull used the same meters we used to show simultaneously the currents in different parts of the circuit, and it was found that the eye could simultaneously see all values as they varied in time. A further advantage of these meters is that one can "add" two current values by translating one of the meters so as to fasten its reference line at the circle of the other meter, thus in effect adding the two displacements. This construction was used to demonstrate Kirchhoff's current law by showing that all of the currents into a node of the circuit always summed to zero. All of the experimental movies have been fashionéd to be presented without sound and to tell their story iconically, in so far as possible. Of course, one may add sound if desired, but by first attempting to construct a computer pantomime, one must face the iconic problem.

Figures VII-1A and 1B show 24 frames selected from the "Dynamic Symbols" film. (The reproduced frames give a very good description of the film's content and should be read from left to right by rows. Near the bottom of some of the frames is the English text that was spoken during one field test to describe what was being shown.) This short film illustrates how computer-generated film can contribute to field-testing and validation of iconic messages.

This 3-1/2 minute film contains three major concepts. It proceeds without using words or mathematical symbols to show that:

This 3-1/2 minute film contains three major concepts. It proceeds without using words or mathematical symbols to show that:

1) The notion that in a system some elements are active (sources) while other elements are passive (inert) until connected to a source. Flow occurs along closed paths through active elements.

2) If more than one path is available, the flow may divide between alternate paths; all the flow will go through a perfect bypass.

3) The topological arrangement of elements influences how the flow is distributed. If two elements are arranged side by side (in parallel) the flow divides between them (not necessarily equally). If two elements are arranged in series, the same flow must necessarily pass through both.

The first field test of this film was designed to inquire whether these basic concepts were intelligibly communicated to college students having no background in engineering, or even whether the film could convey information at all. The film was shown to a class in Introductory Sociology without any explanation as to what it was about. Subsequently the students were asked to describe in their own words what meaning they saw in the successive scenes. It turned out that these nonengineering students were perceiving many of the basic concepts contained in the film although they lacked an appropriate vocabulary to describe them in customary terms. (The average score on concept comprehension was 6.3 out of 12). Many students interpreted the first concept in terms of a boy (active) trying to communicate with his girl (passive). It is rather remarkable that students who interpreted the iconic message in this anthropomorphic way nevertheless learned concept 3) from the film. A second field test, conducted with students (N=68) who were almost all majors in electrical engineering enrolled in an evening course in circuit theory, led to higher concept comprehension (7.7 out of 12), and significantly, nearly all students interpreted the film in electric circuit terms.

The third trial of "Dynamic Symbols" was set up as an experiment to try to evaluate the effect of presenting information via moving symbols (in movies) rather than presenting the same information without motion (in slides). For this experiment a large undergraduate class in Computer Arts and Science

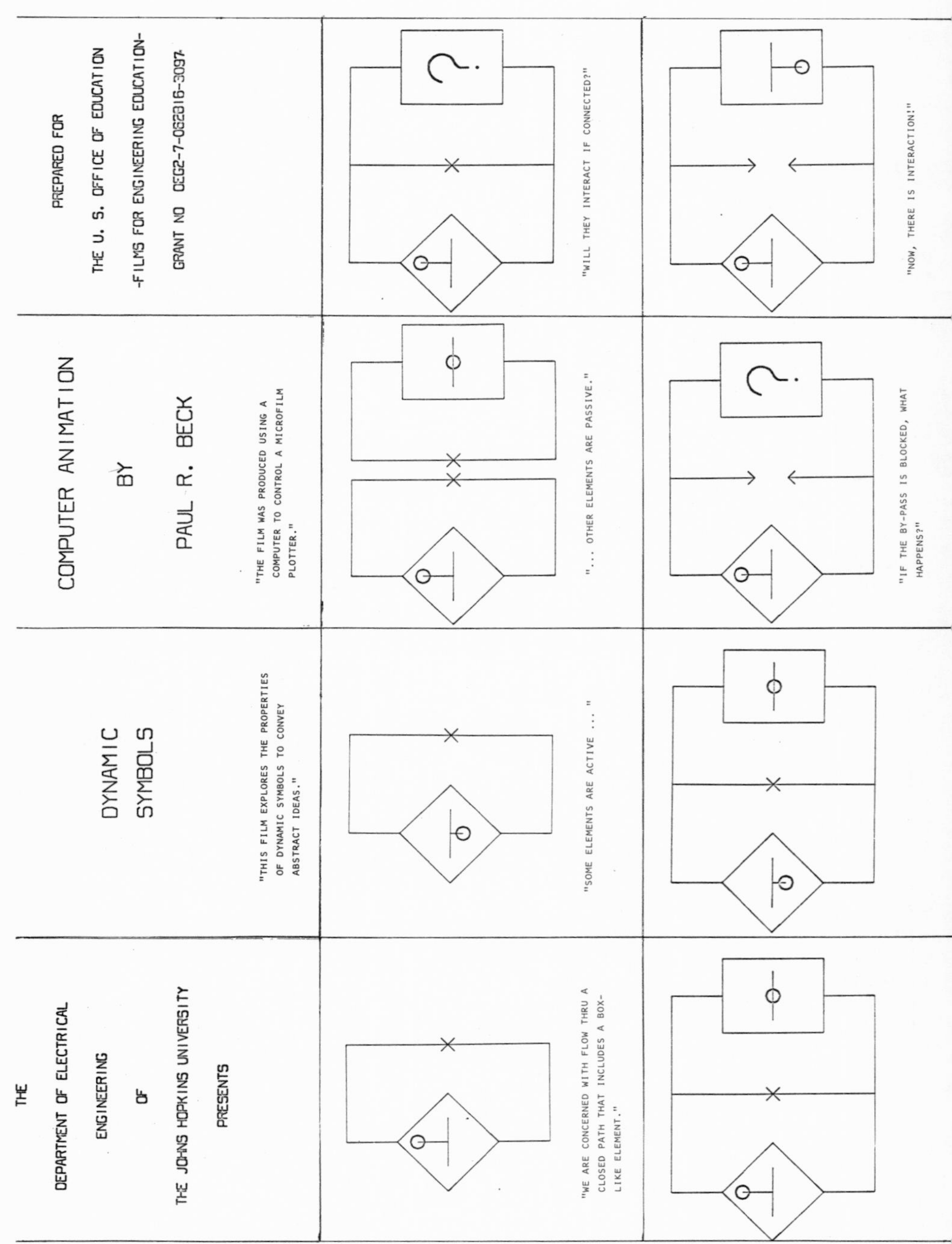

Figure VII-1A, VII-1B. Dynamic Symbols

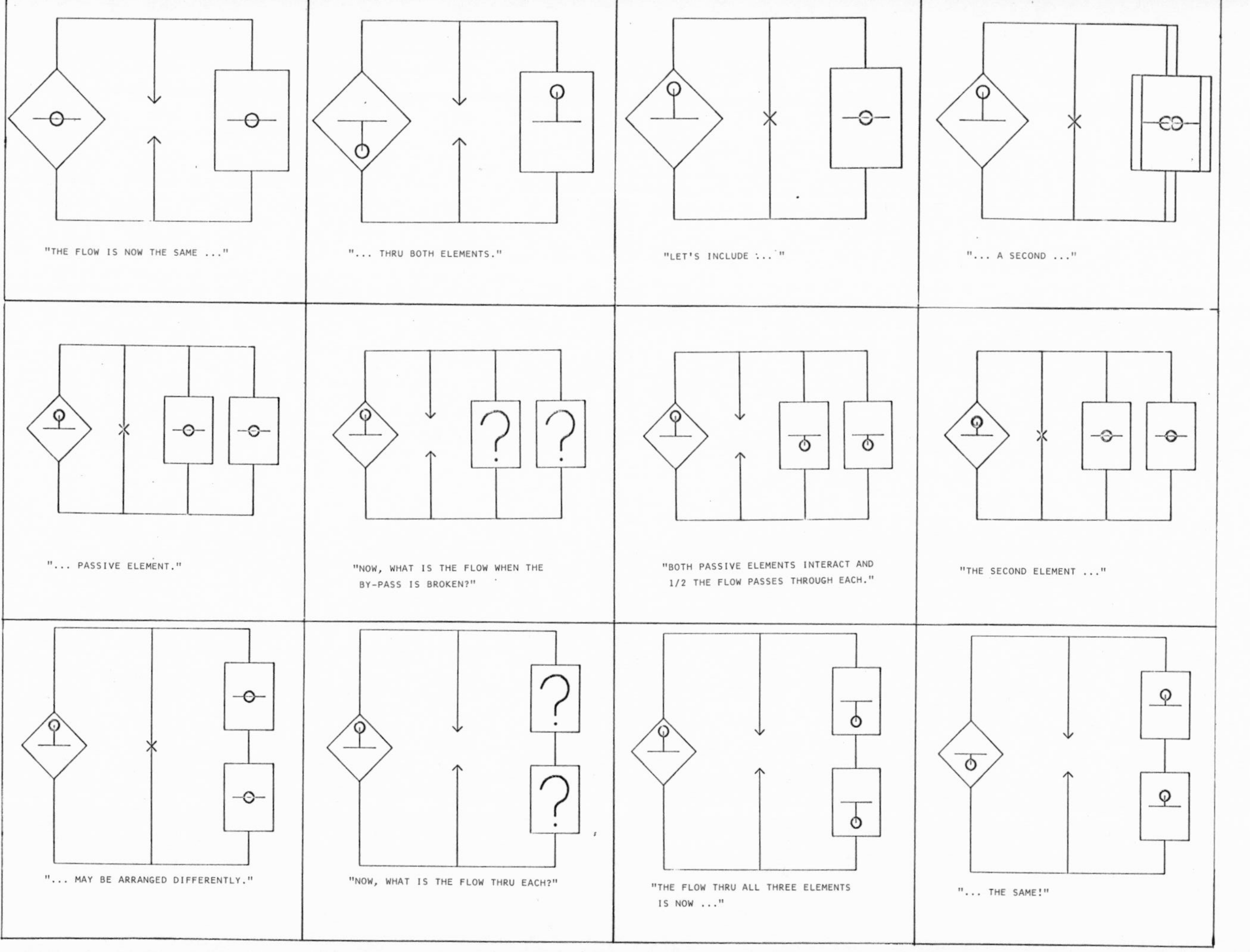
"THE FLOW IS NOW THE SAME ..."
"... THRU BOTH ELEMENTS."
"LET'S INCLUDE ..."
"... A SECOND ..."
"... PASSIVE ELEMENT."
"NOW, WHAT IS THE FLOW WHEN THE BY-PASS IS BROKEN?"
"BOTH PASSIVE ELEMENTS INTERACT AND 1/2 THE FLOW PASSES THROUGH EACH."
"THE SECOND ELEMENT ..."
"... MAY BE ARRANGED DIFFERENTLY."
"NOW, WHAT IS THE FLOW THRU EACH?"
"THE FLOW THRU ALL THREE ELEMENTS IS NOW ..."
"... THE SAME!"

was randomly divided into two groups. One group (N=48) was shown the film, and the other group (N=49) was shown a sequence of motionless slides taken directly from the movie and each displayed for ten seconds (see Fig. VII-1). The same recorded commentary accompanied both the movie and slide presentations. (The text of this commentary is that given at the bottom of each frame in Fig. VII-2). After film or slides was presented, a questionnaire covering the content of each of the scenes I through XI comprising the film was filled out by the students.

Out of a possible score of 18 items of information, the students viewing the film scored 13.2 while those viewing the slides scored 10.7. A t-test of this difference shows it to be significant beyond the .01 level. It seems that adding the property of motion changed the information presented--for instance the concept of flow was more often achieved by students viewing the movie than by students seeing pictures without motion. If students are divided into those scoring above and below average on the post-test, one mode of presentation (slides) is equally effective for all major fields whereas the other mode (films) is noticeably superior in communicating concepts to science and engineering majors. These data are shown below.

	Slides			Film		
Test Scores	Lib Arts	Sci	Engr	Lib Arts	Sci	Engr
Above Average	9	3	5	4	20	6
Below Average	6	8	7	9	6	3
	(Chi^2 = 1.40)			(Chi^2 = 7.96)		

Figure VII-2. Comparison of Slides and Film vs Student Types

Put another way, these data show that an improved mode of presentation will aid those students who are ready to assimilate the information. However, it also suggests that dynamic motion is more meaningful to students in engineering and science whereas liberal arts students appeared to get most of their information from the verbal commentary. (Whether this sense of dynamics is a concomitant trait that leads to an interest in science and engineering -- is an interesting question worthy of further study).

Computer Pantomimes.

Our interest in iconic communication grew from early efforts to makė several educational films which explained various abstract mathematical ideas iconically without the assistance of traditional titles or spoken commentary and mathematical symbolism. The first film HARMONIC PHASORS -- I in a preliminary version by Huggins consisted of many explanatory titles. Subsequently, Weiner suggested a number of improvements and, from these discussions, it was agreed to replace the explanatory titles by iconic expositions derived solely from the visual schemes of the film (HUGGINS 1966).

This effort to make the imagery tell its own story without reliance upon the usual words or mathematical equations soon revealed that one word is worth a thousand pictures. We quickly came to appreciate how dependent is the customary graphical communication upon ordinary language and mathematical conventions.

We called these animated films "computer pantomimes' and have ever since been fascinated and challenged by the problems that arise when the crutch of symbolic language is thus set aside so that one is forced to communicate iconically through appropriate motion and dynamic development of visual schemes. We know of no exercise so effective for heightening one's appreciation for the underdeveloped, atrophied condition of his own iconic skills as the making of a computer pantomime.

Subsequently, we learned of an early famous effort to communicate geometrical concepts iconically which resulted in a set of 22 short films "Visual Geometry" (NICOLET 0000). If these little wordless lessons in geometrical construction and form had been done by computer rather than by hand animation, they would be computer pantomimes of the first rank. Unfortunately, the available prints of these films today are of very poor quality. A meritorious undertaking for students (or professionals) interested in developing their skills in computer animation would be to "reconstruct" these important Nicolet films.

Although we believe that computer pantomimes could be valuable adjuncts to the educational process by demonstrating the structural meaning of ideas and concepts, we doubt that in our present culture they well be widely accepted for a number of reasons. The major obstacle is the paucity of iconic conventions for portraying the most elemental relations and properties of the content of mathematics and physics.

In the drawing of cartoons, many conventions have been established and are well interpreted by the viewer without conscious effort. For instance, a light bulb is sometimes used to suggest that the cartoon character has just gotten a "bright idea." When he is frightened, his hair is shown standing on end. Many other visual conventions of this sort have long been used and have in effect been incorporated into our common language, albeit iconic rather than verbal (see LEVITAN 1960 and GOMBRICH 1969). However, for the most part, these widely accepted iconic conventions do not pertain to the abstract ideas of mathematics and physics.

Each field of science has its own visual schemes and representations, but these are often designed to supplement and clarify aspects of the symbolic (mathematical or verbal) description, rather than to portray directly significant aspects of the phenomena under consideration. Because visual expressions are considered to be subordinate to the symbolic description, the few well-established schemes of graphs, vector diagrams, etc are accepted without exploring if they might be improved or replaced by better schemes. Most visual schemes used today are static forms, appropriate for the printed page, which do not make use of motion and the freedom for generating and displaying sequential relations now available in computer-animated displays. Perhaps, after a few generations of children have grown up watching Sesame Street, The Electric Company and whatever may follow, better iconic conventions for showing the basic ideas of mathematics and physics will be commonplace. But much creative invention is needed.

In representing physical systems, one must show the relationships between the values of the physical observables (ie signals) associated with the system. We have described elsewhere (HUGGINS 1968) the design of a iconic "lollipop" symbol for showing the value of an observable (such as current, voltage, temperature, pressure, etc) at each point in the system. We believe that this visual convention of using the displacement of a mark from its "equilibrium" position provides a simple and useful way of indicating the value of a signal. But for showing the relation between various signals, conventions are almost completely lacking. For instance, to show that one signal is the "cause" and another the "effect" can be done easily only if the "cause" preceeds the "effect" in time. Perhaps causality in physical systems implies no more nor less than just this temporal ordering. Yet, in conceptualizing the relations between various signals, it may be convenient to think of one of them as the cause and another as the effect, even if there is no time ordering. How to show iconically this causal relation? The studies of Michotte (1963) suggest that this may be an unsolvable problem in general.

In developing a computer pantomime, it is necessary to define a new iconic construct using what has previously been defined. It is in this sense that we find that one word is worth a thousand pictures. For instance, in HARMONIC PHASORS to replace the title "phasors add like vectors" by an appropriate iconic explication, required the development of several successive animated sequences showing what is meant by "vector addition."

This and similar subsequent experiences has made us acutely aware of how dependent we are on traditional language when designing movies and other visual representations. We introduce explanatory words in the sound track or accompanying title of a film to not only "explain" but also to prevent "misinterpretation" of what is shown. Because this crutch is so easily and naturally accessible, the author is denied the necessity and discipline of facing fully the iconic problems inherent in his work. As a consequence, the development of more effective iconic schemes is handicapped. We wonder if the designers of the animated sequences in Sesame Street have sought to make these images convey the desired concept even when the sound is turned off? It seems to us that an iconic statement should insofar as possible stand on its own feet. Then, when supplemented by explanatory language, it will represent the concept most strongly.

The over-reliance on accompanying written or spoken description not only denies the author the opportunities to improve his visual explication but it also makes the interpretation of its meaning by the viewer dependent upon the viewer's understanding of the language used. If he does not undertand the language, or if he misunderstands the meaning of what is said, he may be worse off than if he had paid attention only to the visual components. Thus, the crutch of language in supplementing visual display is accompanied by a hazard for both the author and the viewer. In contrast by not depending upon language, a computer pantomime can show and explain a concept without demanding special linguistic skills of its viewers.

Without ordinary language to qualify, interpret, and explain the visual image, one must face a host of problems of a different genre than those associated with writing ordinary text. These involve the management of the visual media in ways that simply do not exist for printed text or spoken language. Whereas a book is printed and completed before being seen by the reader, a movie is seen in real time by the viewer as it develops. Since he does not have the opportunity to review what has gone before (as is easily done in reading the printed page) the timing and sequencing of the elements in a movie scene are of critical importance. Ambiguities that may mislead the viewer into an incorrect line of thought are much more serious than in a printed book where the reader can pause to correct his misconceptions.

In designing an animated film, one encounters many major problems which for the most part do not arise in the mechanical preparation of written text. These involve:

1) Layout of images on screen,
2) Identification and portrayal of relations,
3) Avoidance of irrelevant or wrong information,
4) Use (or misuse) of color,
5) Use of motion and spatial perspective,
6) Invention and design of glyphs

To illustrate the subtle nature of some of these difficulties, we would like to discuss the third problem: the avoidance of irrelevant or misinformation. The subtle yet pervasive nature of this problem was first brought to our attention by Bruce Cornwell when he spoke at our seminar on 23 October 1969. We are indebted to this skilled professional film-maker, who has made many beautiful educational films using hand-animation as well as computer-animation techniques, for these and other insights (see CORNWELL 1970).

Cornwell asked how one might make a film to show how to bisect a given line segment. The immediate suggestion of the participants in the seminar was to produce a animated sequence patterned after the familiar construction using a protractor that every school boy knows, as illustrated in Fig VII-3.

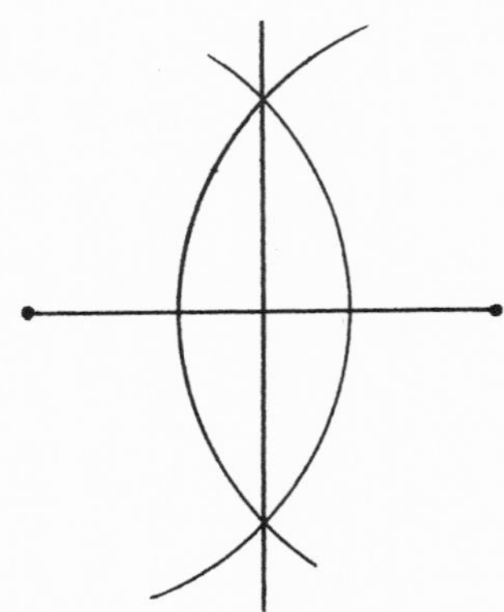

Figure VII-3 Perpendicular Bisector of a Line Segment.

Then Cornwell proceeded to show how faulty such a sequence would be. Since this is a scene from an animated movie, the diagram must evolve in time. The line segment can pop onto the screen initially. Then the two curved arcs should appear as if drawn in turn by the protractor. But now we encounter the first irrelevancy -- in what order should the two arcs be drawn? Should the left arc be drawn before the right arc?

Clearly, to draw one arc before the other introduces irrelevant and misleading information. There is no reason why one should have priority over the other -- to draw one arc before the other is a kind of misinformation than can needlessly puzzle the viewer and deflect his attention from the intended idea. Thus, both arcs must be drawn simultaneously in keeping with Leibniz' principle of sufficient reason (BIRKHOFF 1943).

But still many unanswered questions remain. Should the arcs be drawn in the clockwise or the counterclockwise direction? Clearly, here again, to do either will convey some misinformation since the underlying idea to be communicated is independent of the direction in which the arcs are drawn.

How is the viewer to know that the arcs are segments of two circles whose centers are at the endpoints of the lines being bisected?

How is the viewer to know that the radii of the two arcs are indeed equal?

How to communicate the awareness thât this construction will define the bisector regardless of the radii of the two arcs (provided the radii are sufficiently large that the arcs intersect in two points)?

The iconic answer to these questions is to replace the arcs by two complete growing circles which are launched simultaneously from the end points of the line segment, like two circular ripples propagating outward from two pebbles dropped in a placid pond. The perpendicular bisector is then the locus of the intersection of these two growing circles.

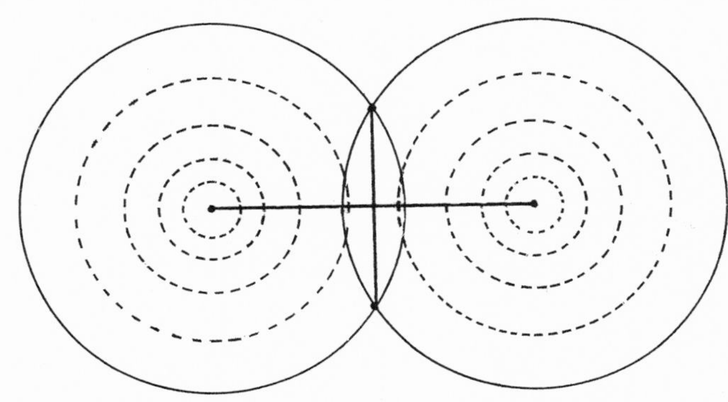

Figure VII-4. Growing Circles.

This solution satisfies Leibniz principle of sufficient reason in that all symmetries are preserved. Furthermore, by allowing the circles to grow from the endpoints, viewers automatically will perceive them to be circles (for who hasn't spent hours watching circular ripples in a pond?). Furthermore, since there is no reason for believing that one circle should be growing more rapidly than the other, the notion of equal radii is maintained. And since the radii increase indefinitely, the result is seen as being independent of the particular radii chosen.

It should be mentioned that in 1971 Charles Kilgus extended this simple idea by showing that by introducing a constant time lag between the instant at which the two growing circles were launched from their respective end points, their intersections generate all of the conic sections. Thus, just as the circle, ellipse, and hyperbola were all related into a single construct by viewing these two-dimensional figures as cross sections of a three-dimensional conic solid, so also, by introducing time as a third dimension, one can generate them as intersections of two dynamic circles. (A computer pantomime showing this is being made by an undergraduate Timothy Cole at Johns Hopkins University).

Face Mnemonics

The use of drawings of faces whose features vary to represent information was proposed by Chernoff (1971). Production of such faces and the study of their information-bearing capacity is a topic of current research at Johns Hopkins by Robert Jacob, Howard Egeth, and W.H. Huggins. The faces are produced by computer graphic methods and, like Weaver's stimuli, are an example of computer-produced stimuli for use in psychological experiments. (See Fig. IV-1).

A single drawing of a face can be represented by a point in a multidimensional space. Equivalently, it can represent a collection of data by considering the constituent data to be the coordinates of the point in this space (ie the collection of data may be regarded as the components of a multidimensional vector). In this way, the facial features are determined by the n coordinates of the point in a n-dimensional space. Presently faces are being constructed which contain features varying according to 19 independent parameters, such as height of nose, slant of eyes, location of "dimple," and the like. A particular dimension is associated with each parameter.

Many different faces can be drawn consistent with data represented in a multidimensional space. Each type of parametric variation in the faces is determined by and related to the variation along one dimension. The faces consist of segments of ellipses, circles, and straight lines. Since conic sections can be described by simple equations related to the values of the coordinates of a point in the multidimensional space, a digital computer can be instructed to drive a plotter yielding drawings of faces.

This particular scheme for iconic communication with people seems to be especially effective because humans are experienced at recognizing and examining human faces. Even young children can distinguish among large sets of faces after short viewing times (FEINMAN 1973). As Chernoff (1971 pp 15-16) says:

> People grow up studying and reacting to faces all of the time. Small and barely measurable differences are easily detected and evoke emotional reactions from a long catalogue buried in the memory. Relatively large differences go unnoticed in circumstances where they are not important... P articularly valuable is this flexibility in disregarding non-informative data and searching for useful information...
>
> The ability to relate faces to emotional reactions seems to carry a mnemonic advantage... Certain major characteristics of the faces are instantly observed and easily remembered in terms of emotions and appearance. Finer details and correlations become apparent after studying the faces for a time. The awareness of these does not drive

out of mind the original major impressions.

Evidence from developing infants suggests that face-like objects are responded to within the first weeks of life and that by six months infants respond differentially to the mother's face. Since faces are complex in informational terms, the use of facial nuances to display complex information seems natural. The research of Jacob et al aims at investigating the feasibility of "facial" coding.

Another use for computer-generated faces is in the psychological study of perception. Perceptual experiments have long relied on stimuli such as photographs of models, crude drawings, and the like, even though such stimuli are necessaruly crude in precision and richness. Drawings, for example, have rarely dealt with stimuli varying in more than three or four clearly definable dimensions. Computer-generated faces appear to provide a source of rich, precisely controllable iconic images useful as stimuli in perception research.

The two strands of research are mutually dependent. Effective use of face mnemonics for iconic communication will require precise psychological research addressing perceptual issues, but perceptual issues in turn require analysis in information-theoretic terms of properties of the faces.

Some experiments now in progress are investigating whether faces are indeed a good representation for arbitrary (in particular, uncorrelated multivariate uniform random) data, compared both to symbolic representation and to alternate iconic schemes. Hopefully this approach will domonstrate the validity of the "facial" method of iconic communication. A subsequent step will involve how best to use the faces to study sets of data. Is the information communicated reasonably constant regardless of the way in which the facial features are related to the data?

The parameters which presently account for variation in constructed faces locate a face in a primal 19-dimensional Euclidian space (the space in which the original data points exist). However, the construction of the faces involves the parameters in a somewhat interdependent way--the size and curvature of the mouth are clearly related; or the size of the eyes and the size of the pupils are related, so that if the eyes are small, the pupils are less prominant. Furthermore, some parameters are more important than others (eg the outline of the face maybe more crucial than the location of the mouth). Thus a 19-dimensional Euclidian space may not be the most meaningful nor efficient representation since the face does not in fact vary in 19 orthogonal and equally important ways.

One can imagine a subjective perceptual feature subspace of less than 19 dimensions with oblique axes embedded within the primal space. The 19 dimensions of the primal space are themselves without intrinsic uniqueness, being arbitrary choices selected by the programmer who wrote the computer graphics program. A better choice of axes would be to choose directions that correspond to the various attributes that people by and large perceive in facial features. Fortunately, it may be possible by methods akin to factor analysis to determine experimentally what these more appropriate axes are. Then the parameter set characterizing the face may be redefined to correspond to these natural directions, thus permitting the data to be encoded in naturally discriminable ways.

Study of the perception of the faces may yield information about the nature of perceptual and cognitive spaces. Experimental results can provide clues about the nature of these spaces, the nature of the transformations between them and, hence, potentially shed light on the process of perception of iconic information. Conversely, investigation of the transformations from the formal space to the perceptual space and to the individual's cognitive space will provide information about both the perceptual process itself and about how iconic communication may be most effective. Aspects of the cognitive space which are pertinent and relatively invariant over individuals may be a key determinant of effective iconic communication schemes.

Weaver's Stimuli

In 1970 Garner proposed a rationale to account for how human beings rate patterns. He noted that patterns receiving the highest ratings in terms of "goodness" were arrangements where patterns would change least under various kinds of transformations--rotations, reflections, and others. The pattern shown in Fig. VII-5a below is symmetric, while that shown in Fig. VII-5b is not symmetric.

Fig. VII-5a Fig. VII-5b Fig. VII-5c

To Garner, however, Fig. VII-5a which subjects judge as a better pattern than Fig. VII-5b, has the important property that it is unchanged by a reflection around a horizontal axis. Fig. VII-5b, on the other hand yields different pattern when reflected (Fig. VII-5c).

Weaver at Johns Hopkins is currently extending Garner's two-dimensional investigations to 3-dimensional patterns. Before beginning the three-dimensional study, he investigated the effect of closure when applied to the two-dimensional dot patterns used by Garner by enclosing each dot pattern in the smallest convex polygon which would just cover the pattern of dots. The resulting convex polygons are subject to the same set of transformations as the original dot patterns.

Under closure neither the interior point on the grid nor the middle point of any three collinear points supplies any information about the structure of the polygon. Hence closure reduces the number of patterns in the polygon space. Without closure the number of independent dot patterns is 17, yielding a population of 90 unique patterns via rotation and reflection transformations. With closure there are 15 independent polygons with a population of 74 unique patterns derivable from transformations.

Following the method of Garner and Clement (1963), Weaver asked subjects to rate patterns in terms of "goodness," using a scale from 1 to 17 (ranking task). Then he asked different subjects to group patterns into subsets, so that subsets would contain items that closely resembled one one another (grouping task). The two sets of subjects thus performed two tasks for dot patterns and for closure patterns. One group ranked the patterns, the other group grouped patterns.

PRELIMINARY CORRELATION SUMMARIES.

Stimuli Used	Subject Ranking vs Subject Grouping	Subject Ranking vs Objective Set Size
Dot Patterns	.75	.79
Closure Patterns	.90	.78

Although the correlations are not as strong as some published by Garner and his colleagues, these results do confirm earlier findings. Of special interest is the correlation for polygonal stimuli. Note that there is a higher correlation between ranking of goodness with the subject grouping than with the set size. It appears that some subjects (both raters and groupers) include the perspective transformation (determined by their point of view) and view these polygons as perspective pictures of wire-frame objects in three-space. Evidence of this is found in the fact that the trapezoids are often rated and grouped with squares. Such grouping does not correspond exactly with the objective set determined by the original set of transformations which partition the pattern space.

In light of recent work of Shepard and Cermak (1973) with toroidal sets of free-form stimuli, it is reasonable to hypothesize that the viewer uses a basic set of primitive objects which he mentally manipulates by perspective scaling under translation and then combines these modified primitives to approximate a perceived pattern. Trapezoids can be interpreted as views of squares in perspective and since the square primitive is a highly redundant pattern, these trapezoids are grouped with squares and rated high in goodness.

Both aspects of this hypothesis, transformations on the primitive objects and alteration of the subject's viewpoint, can be investigated analytically using the theory developed by

Roberts (1963) in his study of machine perception of three-dimensional objects. Since preliminary data suggest that the subject's viewpoint enters into pattern evaluation, it is meaningful to investigate whether the basic hypothesis (that good patterns have few alternatives) holds for three-dimensional stimuli where the viewpoint of the observer in relation to the object cannot be ignored and must be definitely treated as one of the experimental variables.

It seems natural to investigate the family of 3-dimensional patterns constructed in an analogous manner to that used to construct the 2-dimensional patterns since human visual stimuli normally occur in a 3-space. (The importance of this is underlined by subjects' tendency to cast even 2-dimensional objects in a 3-dimensional context (ie trapezoids are seen as squares in perspective). A procedure for finding all three-dimensional patterns which can be related by a set of rigid rotation and reflection transformations is needed. Weaver has used group-theoretic methods to partition the pattern space into its relatives. This theory yields a measure of the set size which, according to the Garnerian hypothesis, is inversely related to pattern "goodness."

This group-theoretic technique will partition the two- and three-dimensional dot or closure patterns. When the operation of closure is applied to three-dimensional dot patterns one obtains convex polyhedra which can be used as stimuli to investigate the perception of the "goodness' of three-dimensional patterns.

Weaver placed 10 dots on a 3x3x3 lattice with the restriction that no row column or layer be empty. The group-theoretic procedure enables one to reduce the 270 possible dot assignments which satisfy this restriction to just 15 independent dot patterns by applying group rotation and reflection transformations that leave the three-dimensional grid invariant. If these dot patterns are enclosed in minimal convex polyhedra, one obtains 226 polyhedra which can be derived from 14 independent polyhedra by the same set of transformations.

Stereographic projections of these polyhedra are presented to the subject the viewer's position affects his assessment of pattern "goodness," some criterion for picking a particular viepoint was needed. This was done by selecting that particular viewpoint which maximized the least separation between the lattice lines when projected onto the picture plane. This choice maximizes the discriminability of the nodes and, hence, the information from the grid.

Two presentations of these patterns are being investigated. First, stereographic pictures with the hidden edges of the polyhedra suppressed where the subject is asked to rate the pattern for "goodness." Second, the same polytopes are used with the hidden edges shown by broken lines. A comparison of the ratings of these two presentations provides a means to investigate how the viewer fills in the hidden lines when they are not explicitly shown. The hypothesis is that he supplies the missing information so as to maximize the goodness of the resulting polytope.

To prepare such perspective drawings of the stimuli without using computer graphics would be technically most difficult and not feasible economically. However three-dimensional graphic and vector routines (such as those which have been incorporated in M*O*G*U*L by Huggins and Weaver) provide an efficient and relatively inexpensive method for generating the thousands of stimulus slides used in Weaver's study.

A further fundamental study now made possible by these technological advances, involves the effect of motion on perceived pattern "goodness." With the aid of computer-graphic programs, perspective pictures of three-dimensional wire-frame models with hidden edges removed can be generated and subjected to rotation and/or translation. Thus, one can simulate the images the subject would see if he slowly changed his viewpoint and examined the entire surface of the polyhedron. Ratings for patterns obtained using such dynamic displays could then be compared with ratings from static displays and the significance of motion evaluated. Weaver is currently exploring moving stimuli using a computer-generated movie of moving polyhedra in three-space.

VIII. REFERENCES -- FORMAT AND DESCRIPTION.

This bibliography was prepared using the Information Storage Package at the Johns Hopkins Medical Institutions Computing System. The data were entered by cards punched on an IBM-026 key punch, as were also various editing changes. We are grateful for the help and advise given us by Dr. Richard Shepard and Joyce Ward who helped us over various transitions from the IBM-360/91 computer (on which we began) to the CDC-3300 computer (on which most of the work was done) to, finally, the IBM-370/145 computer (on which this final version was prepared).

In retrospect, it is doubtful that the use of the computer saved time and effort. But hope springs eternal. We at least now have the text and bibliography in machine-readable form (9-track magnetic tape in EBCDIC code) and expect to be able to carry out future editings using our PDP-11/45 scope terminal. For the cost of handling, we will copy this tape upon request if a blank (2400-ft) reel is provided.

Each bibliographic item is a separate record with the margins, indentation, justification, and pagination being accomplished by a PRINT program which is governed by a set of print parameters (set by special format records) and a reserved "new-line" character.

The descriptors (given between virgules in most of the bibliographic items) permit this tape to be scanned by a SEARCH program to retrieve those items which satisfy various logical combinations of descriptors. A standard file consists of records up to 10,000 characters long, the last record being followed by a file mark. Each record consists of a 5-digit record number, followed by two format control characters (for use by the PRINT program), followed by the text of the record, followed by a terminal dollar sign. Hence, anyone wishing to work with this text should find it possible to translate the file into the particular format required by his own text-processing system.

Each bibliography item may be composed of up to 8 subitems, some of which may be missing. Each subitem begins on a new line and ends with a period. The items are entered in the specific order given by the example below.

1. Designator. SMITH 1956.
2. Author. John W. Smith.
3. Title. Symbol manipulation languages.
4. Source. Communications of the ACM 10(1967)793-799,803.

5. Abstract. This is text of abstract. (Number of references-). Abstract by author.

6. Citations. /*ROSENFELD 1969/*SMITH 1956A/.

7. Descriptors. /1967/SMITH/WHH/film/education/perception/psychology/.

8. Comments. READER'S COMMENTS -- This paper is not relevant except for one germ of an idea -- that is... .

The following description gives first the general format of the final printing.

1. Designator Use uppercase letters, with only last name of author, single space, year, period, viz.

SMITH 1956.

To distinguish between two or more authors with the same last name, append to the last name a comma and the author's initials without periods and without spaces,

SMITH,JW 1956.

To distinguish between two or more publications by the same author in a given year, append to the date the upper-case letters A, B, C, ..., viz.

SMITH,JW 1956A.
SMITH,JW 1956B.

2. Author Here list in full with first name first and full punctuation as

John W. Smith.

In case of multiple authors, list them in order given in the publication. However, make a designator for each author. That is

R.L. Adler and A.G. Konheim.

will require two designators (the second to be treated as an additional bibliographic item and entered as

KONHEIM 1962
A.G. Konheim -- see ADLER 1962.

3. Title — The title is given with only the first letter capitalized, except for proper names, viz.

Symbol manipulation languages.

4. Source — Standard bibliographic ordering is journal volume(year) pages, viz.

Communications of the ACM 10(1967) 793-799.

5. Abstract — Give here the abstract and the author of the abstract (if known) and also show number of references to other papers included in the paper, viz.

Xxxxxxxxxxxxxxxxxxxxxxxxxxxxxxxxxxxxxxxxx-xxxxxxxxxxxxxxxxxxxxxxxxxxxxxxxxx xxxxxxxxxxx-x

xxxxxxxxxxxxxxxxxxxxxxxxxxxxxxxxxxxxxxxxxx-xxxxxxxxxxxxxxxxxxxxx xxxxxxxxxxxxxxxxxxxxxxx-xxxx,(46 references). (Abstract by author).

6. Citations — These are the designators of other references that have cited this item. Although listed separately from the descriptors, the citations are given in the form of descriptors as

/*DESIGNATOR/

with the designator preceded by an asterisk and enclosed between virgules, viz.

/*ROSENFELD 1969/*SMITH 1956A/.

7. Descriptors — The first three descriptors should give in standard order the date, the last name of each author, and the bibliographer's initials. Then, following this are whatever keywords and descriptors seem appropriate for the item, all in lower case except for proper names.

/1967/JONES/SMITH/WHH/film/perception/psychology/education/.

Caution should be taken to avoid inadvertently including a blank space in a descriptor as this will yield a different character string. Also, consistency is essential in punctuation and capitalization.

8. Comments Here go any comments the bibliographer cares to make about this item. These comments may be made liberally since they will be reviewed and edited to decide which comments should appear in the final listing for publication.

Persons contributing to the bibliography are

KMB.....Kenneth M. Bakalar.
TWB.....Thomas W. Balma.
JRB.....James R. Bennett.
NDB.....Nicholas D. Beser.
DRE.....Doris R. Entwisle.
PKF.....Paul K. Fessler.
MHG.....Mark H. Goldstein.
DBH.....Douglas B. Helmuth.
WHH.....William H. Huggins.
RJJ.....Robert J. Jacob.
DJK.....David J. Kasik.
CCK.....Charles C. Kilgus.
WEK.....William E. Knannlein.
PMK.....Peter M. Kuzmak.
DJM.....David J. Mishelevich.
IDS.....Ian D. Smith.
JWW.....John W. Weaver.
DGW.....Donald G. Wilson.
SMZ.....Stephen M. Zwarg.

AHUJA 1968.
D.V. Ahuja and S.A. Coons.
Geometry for construction and display.
IBM Systems Journal 7(1968)188-205.

This paper and the companion paper on "An algorithm for generating spline-like curves" in the same issue offers a tutorial exposition of the use of homogeneous coordinates and provides a very helpful discussion to explain the extremely abreviated treatment given by Roberts (1966).

/1968/AHUJA/COONS/WHH/geometry/spatial/theory/display/.

ALLEN 1971.
William H. Allen.
Instructional media research past, present and future.
AV Communication Review 19(1971)5-18.

This paper reviews educational media research starting before 1950 to the present. "Evaluative comparisions" for 30 years prior to 1950 showed films and other audiovisual presentations to be superior to the "usual method of instruction". Between 1945 and 1955, military studies approached problems in media research via a systematic and programmatic perspective. No implementation of this research was forthcoming, however. From 1955 to 1965, attention was directed at educational TV, and again evaluation was a major theme. Similar remarks apply to programmed instruction. At present media research is characterized by (1) Study of the 3-way interaction of stimulus, task and learner, (2) Research on structure and sequencing of instruction, (3) Emphasis on "systems' but little actual research, (4) Little attention to related matters such as psychometric applications or equipment design. The author sees de-emphasis of small-scale studies and experiments in the future in favor of large-scale applied and developmental projects. There are 37 references.

/1971/ALLEN/DRE/instructional media/.

READER'S COMMENTS -- This is a discursive paper reviewing the present state-of-the-art in media research. The author does not mention computer-generated films nor the possibilities that this medium offers for precisely controlled studies.

ANDERSON,CM 1972.
Charles M. Anderson.
In search of a visual rhetoric for instructional television.
AV Communication Review 20(1972)43-63.

This paper discusses the lack of superior learning from instructional television, putting aside its logical advantages. Much empirical work is summarized on effects of visualization, camera factors,motion, and color. One conclusion is that the majority of studies have not used television as a visual medium but as a pipe line for incidental activities accompanying a verbal presentation. The author advocates a basic change in methodology so that the visual channel is used for presentation of crucial material. There are 40 references.

/1972/ANDERSON/DRE/education/visual/media/.

ANDERSON,SE 1968.
S.E. Anderson -- see WEINER 1968.

ANON 1969.
Anonymous.
The art of motion graphics.
IBM Computing Report (March 1969) 10-13.

/1969/ANCN/SMZ/computer/graphics/art/.

READER'S COMMENTS -- This romantic exposition by an anonymous writer describes the creation of movies by an artist and a scientist working together with an IBM graphics terminal. A program puts patterns on the graphics terminal screen, which the artist can then manipulate. The camera then photographs the screen frame by frame. When the film is run the patterns change and move as they were controlled by the artist. Optical printer processing later introduces color and other effects. The article is a general description of the process and some of its handicaps.

APPEL 1968A.
Arthur Appel.
Modeling in three dimensions.
IBM Systems Journal 7(1968) 310-321.

Discussed are two computer programs for generating and realistically plotting any view of a three-dimensional object from the same object description, thereby simulating the viewpoints of a person moving around the object. Although the programs have been implemented -- on an experimental basis-- for digital plotting, the use of the underlying concepts for graphic display is contemplated.

Involved in the SIGHT program are approaches to some of the most difficult problems in three-dimensional graphics-- the hidden-line problem, approximating curved solids by polyhedra, and simulating degrees of surface transparency.

The description of the program LEGER emphasizes the design of data storage for the object description. This scheme allows the use of the same data for generating all views of the object. The data structure can be modified to adjust the dimensions of the scene and the relative orientations of the component parts. There are nine references. Abstract by author.

/*LOUTREL 1968/

/1968/APPEL/computer/program/geometry/spatial/.

APPEL 1968B.
Arthur Appel.
On calculating the illusion of reality.

IFIP Congress 1968. Booklet E., E79-E84.

The power of the computer can be used to improve as well as to automate the pictures needed for the graphic arts and communication. This paper describes techniques by which the quality of computer generated graphics can be improved in realism. These techniques, applicable to shading, shadow casting, and coloring, have been applied only to scenes which consist of assemblies of polyhedra but nevertheless portend a significant improvement in the graphic capability available to artists and designers. There are five references. Abstract by author.

/*LOUTREL 1968/.

/1968/APPEL/computer/spatial/illusion/program/.

APPEL 1968C.
Arthur Appel.
Shadows without substance: some techniques for shading machine renderings of solids.
Proceedings of the SJCC 32(1968)7-45.

The value of shading a line drawing and indicating the shadows cast is discussed and demonstrated. Previous work in the automatic generation of shaded pictures is reviewed. An algorithm for automatic determination of polyhedral chiaroscuro where the scene is illuminated by an arbitrarily located light source is presented. This technique enables the shading of line drawings of assemblies of polyhedra to be determined in slightly less than the square root of the time required for shading by point by point methods. There are no restrictions on the shapes of polyhedra that may be rendered except that no two polyhedra can intersect or be tangent to each other. There are fifteen references. Abstract by author.

/1968/APPEL/computer/graphics/shading/.

ARNHEIM 1969.
Rudolf Arnheim.
Visual Thinking.
University of Calfornia Press (Berkeley), 1969.

This book concerns visual perception as a cognitive activity. The author asserts that all thinking (not just thinking related to art or other visual experiences) is basically perceptual in nature, and that the ancient dichotomies between seeing and thinking, between perceiving and reasoning, are false. He suggests that even the fundamental processes of vision involve mechanisms typical of reasoning, and he describes problem-solving in the arts as well as imagery in the thought-models of science. Far from being a "lower" function, our perceptual response to the world is the basic means by which we structure events, and from which we derive ideas and therefore language.

Arnheim draws on material from philosophy, psychological experiments, childrens's perception, children's art-work and from scientific writings on physics and astronomy. The book is intended for the general reader, but is especially pertinent for a background in Iconic Communication because it points up the general neglect of iconics while simultaneously documenting the importance of iconics. There are 313 references.

/*PYLYSHYN 1973/.

/1969/ARNHEIM/DRE/iconics/visual/perception/.

ARNOULT 1956.
Malcolm D. Arnoult -- see ATTNEAVE 1956.

ARNOULT 1960.
Malcolm D. Arnoult.
Prediction of perceptual responses for structural characteristics of the stimulus.
Perceptual and Motor Skills 11(1960)261-268.

The problem is to identify stimulus properties that determine perceptual responses. By using nonsense forms and getting subjects to judge the forms' familiarity, meaningfulness, size, and complexity, the author is able to get multiple correlations between physical measures (perimeter, area, etc.) and the judged properties (familiarity, etc.). Over 80 percent of the variance can be accounted for. There are twelve references.

/1960/ARNOULT/DRE/psychology/perception/physical/structure/stimulus/.

READER'S COMMENTS -- This approach to the problem seems to me to be singularly unimaginative and lacking in theoretical context.

ATKINSON 1973.
Janette Atkinson -- see EGETH 1973.

ATTNEAVE 1956.
Fred Attneave and Malcolm D. Arnoult.
The quantitative study of shape and pattern perception.
Psychological Bulletin 53(1956)452-471.

Shape is a multidimensional variable. The number of dimensions necessary to describe a shape is not fixed, but increases with the complexity of the shape. Even when, in a particular case, the number of dimensions is known, the choice of particular descriptive terms (i.e. reference axes) remains a problem; presumably some terms are more psychologically meaningful than others. Several methods are given for generating "random shapes' to exemplify classes of shapes which can be constructed. In analysis of natural forms, a technique is needed to specify physical measurements of a psychologically relevant sort, but the symmetric shapes do not necessarily give the statistical parameters needed to link synthetic and natural shapes. Neither do the symmetric shapes tell how to determine or measure the parameters of natural shapes. Work of Rashevsky concerned with psychologically relevant measures of form is summarized. Problems in analysis of contour are discussed. Form perception involves a number of different psychological mechanisms which function in a complementary, and somewhat overlapping way. Only experimentation can determine which physical measurements have greatest psychological relevance. There are 27 references.

/1956/ATTNEAVE/ARNOULT/DRE/psychology/perception/shape/pattern/.

READER'S COMMENTS -- This article raises considerations of great relevance to iconic communication.

ATTNEAVE 1957.
Fred Attneave.
Physical determinants of the judged complexity of shapes.
Journal of Experimental Psychology 53(1957) 221-227.

Random polygons were constructed, and some converted into curved figures. A class of symmetrical figures was also constructed. The following parameters of shape were then varied as in a quasi-factorial design: matrix grain, curvedness, symmetry, number of turns, ratio of perimeter to area, angular variability. Judgments of 72 shapes were obtained from 168 subjects. About 90 percent of variance of subjects' ratings was explained (A) By number of independent turns in the contour, (B) Symmetry (symmetrical shapes were judged more complex than asymmetrical with number of independent turns constant, but less complex with total number of turns constant) and (C) The arithmetic mean of algebraic differences in degrees between successive turns in the contour. Angular and curved shapes were judged about equally complex, though the latter involved additional degrees of freedom (radii of curvature). Immaterial, within broad limits, was the grain of the matrix from which critical points were chosen to construct shapes. There are 11 references.

/1957/ATTNEAVE/DRE/psychology/shape/complexity/.

BAECKER 1969A.
Ronald M. Baecker.
Interactive computer-mediated animation.
Ph.D. Dissertation -- Course VI. Massachusetts Institute of Technology, June 1969.

The use of interactive computer graphics in the construction of animated visual displays is investigated.

The dissertation presents a process called interactive computer-mediated animation, in which dynamic displays are constructed by utilizing direct console commands, algorithms, free-hand sketches, and real-time actions. The resulting "movie" can then be immediately viewed and altered.

The dissertation also describes a special kind of interactive computer-mediated animation that exploits the potentialities of direct graphical interaction. The animator may sketch and refine (1) Static images to be used as components of individual frames of the movie, and (2) Static and dynamic images that represent dynamic behavior, that is, movement and rhythm. Because these latter pictures drive algorithms to generate dynamic displays, the process is called picture-driven animation.

Each representation of movement and rhythm determines critical parameters of a sequence of frames. Thus, with a single sketch or action that generates or modifies the representation, the animator can exercise dynamic control over an entire interval of the movie. One natural way to do this is by mimicking in real time a movement or a rhythm, using a stylus or a push-button.

These concepts are supported by experience with three special-purpose picture-driven animation systems which have been implemented and used on the M.I.T. Lincoln Laboratory TX-2 computer.

The dissertation also presents an outline of the proposed design of a multi-purpose, open-ended, interactive animation and Picture Processing Language. APPL is a conversational language which accepts direct sketches, direct console commands, and algorithms that control interactive dynamic displays.

Solutions are presented for the following problems: how can the system be structured so that the command set can easily be augmented by the animator? How can movie time be represented in the language, and how does the choice of representation interact with the flow of program and system control? What computational data structure can facilitate the modeling of sequential and hierarchic structures of pictures and dynamic data? How can we provide a rich picture description capability in the language? How can we facilitate the construction of programs which describe the user's interaction with the system?

APPL programs are included to demonstrate that the language can be gracefully used to construct dynamic displays, to build system tools that aid the construction process, and to implement special-purpose interactive computer-mediated animation systems. There are 110 references. Abstract by author.

/1969/BAECKER/animation/cinema/language/interactive/computer/.

BAECKER 1969B.
Ronald M. Baecker.
Picture-driven animation.
Bethesda Maryland: National Institute of Health, 1969.

Interactive computer-mediated animation is a process for the construction of animated visual displays. Dynamic displays are specified through a combination of direct console commands, sketches, and algorithms. The resulting "movie" can then be immediately viewed and altered. The paper presents a special kind of interactive computer-mediated animation that particularly exploits the potentialities of direct graphical interaction. This process is called picture-driven animation. The animator may sketch and refine (1) static images to be used as components of individual frames of the movie, and (2) static and dynamic images that represent dynamic behavior, that is movement and rhythm. These latter pictures drive algorithms to generate dynamic displays. There are 34 references. Abstract by author.

/*SUTHERLAND,WR 1969/.

/1969/BAECKER/SMZ/animation/cinema/computer/system/.

READER'S COMMENTS -- The article describes one of the few possible viable systems for computer animation. Given the hardware of a graphics terminal (with an associated computer) and an input device such as a light pen or tablet, and the software GENESYS system, it is possible to create simple animation sequences in other than a frame-by-frame manner. The advantages of this system are that it is interactive (immediate turn-around), it is possible to specify by drawing to the computer what the basic animation elements are, and overall (or global) descriptions of the animation using Path, Selection, and Rhythm Descriptors relieve the user from frame-by-frame specifications. This system is an improvement over the methods using a 7094 computer with SC-4020 microfilm plotter, where turn-around is slow and the user must specify mathematically to the computer (by tables or by calculating algorithms) exactly what is to be drawn. The point of the GENESYS system is to try to get the artist or animator back in the process.

An excellent list of references is included.

BAECKER 1971.
Ronald M. Baecker.
A proposal for a computer animation utility over the ARPA-NET.
Draft.

This paper is a proposal for the design, construction, and initial use of a nationwide computer animation utility. It is to be based on a conversational animation system, GENESYS II, which can be accessed over the ARPA-NET from a variety of terminals and through a variety of written and graphical languages. An expanding library of images, movements, and procedural descriptions of images and movements will be available to all users. Augmenting the animation and library components will be a variety of service facilities for image, audio, film, and video processing.

The major goal of the project is the provision of animation power, access to computer animation systems and facilities for movie production, to educators and researchers located all over the country.

The proposal requests funding for the initial phase of the project: (1) The design and implementation of GENESYS II for use over the ARPA-NET at a variety of graphics terminals; (2) The production of a number of computer-animated movies using this system; and, (3) An evaluation of the feasibility of providing responsive computer animation service over the ARPA-NET. If this proves feasible, a second funding phase will be requested to complete the project. There are no references. Abstract by author.

/1971/BAECKER/KMK/computer/graphics/systems/.

READER'S COMMENTS -- Outlines features of proposed utility, though rather sketchy.

BARACH 1964.
Arnold B. Barach and Rudolf Modley.
USA and its Economic Future.
The 20'th Century Fund, New York, 1964.

/1964/BARACH/MODLEY/WHH/economic/statistics/graphics/communication/.

READER'S COMMENTS -- The use of graphics for conveying economic data. See also the book, Europe and its Economic Future, by the same authors which was published in many European languages.

BARRATT 1953.
P.E. Barratt.
Imagery and thinking.
Australian Journal of Psychology 5(1953) 154-164.

This paper describes the results of an attempt to develop a method for obtaining information on the role of imagery in the solution of problems of various kinds cast in a spatial medium. The basic technique involved obtaining imagery rating responses from subjects after they had taken particular spatial group tests. In all, 23 spatial group tests (of which 12 were included in the final analysis) were administered to a group of volunteer undergraduates of both sexes of New England University College. The number of subjects varied from 40 to 61. After each test subjects were permitted to look back over the test items and to make a rating on imagery as a component of problem solving. Three imagery variables, 1) strength and clearness of images visualization in solution, 2) importance and use of visualizations, 3) facility of manipulation of visualizations were each rated on a scale of 0 to 20 by the subjects after each test. The three scores were added together to give a single image rating per test per subject. Results of pilot studies indicated that the tests could be grouped into one of three factor groupings:

1) Spatial manipulation, in which the tests appeared to require a capacity to manipulate visual-imaginal processes
2) Spatial reasoning
3) Shape recognition, requiring the imaginal holding of shapes or configurations against competing shapes.

Final analysis was based on the results of 12 of the 23 tests which appeared to group naturally into one of the three factor 1 groups. Imagery ratings for the three groups of tests averaged over all subjects established the following rank ordering for imagery over the three groups (scores are out of a possible maximum score of 60)

1) Spatial manipulation (33.95)
2) Shape recognition (28.27)
3) Spatial reasoning (22.83)

Further analysis involved a comparison of subject imagery ratings with test performance. Comparison was made between upper and lower quartiles of imagers, that is, between those generally giving the highest imagery ratings and those giving the lowest. On factor 1 (manipulation) tests, high imagers on the average scored higher on each of the tests, the difference being significant at the 5% level (the average high imager score being 30% higher than the average low imager score). On factor 2 (reasoning) tests, the differences were not considered to be significant (high imagers averaged 4% higher scores). Although high imagers averaged 12% higher scores than low imagers on factor 3 tests, the significance was considered to be somewhat uncertain statistically. The lack of significant differences in factor 2 tests was interpreted as evidence against the premise that subjects who perform well in any group give high imagery ratings. The tentative conclusion reported by the author is that imagery as determined by rating behavior is related to success on some types of spatial tasks but not on others. There are 6 references.

/1953/BARRATT/TWB/mental/imagery/thought/test results/psychology/.

READER'S COMMENTS -- Understanding of the results reported in this paper would be greatly enhanced if the reader had more information on the nature of the psychological tests administered to the subjects.

BAYLOR 1972.
G.W. Baylor.
A treatise on the mind's eye: An empirical investigation of visual imagery.
Doctoral DISSERTATION, Carnegie-Mellon University, Ann Arbor, Michigan: University Microfilms, 1972 No 72-12, 699.

BEATTY 1967.
Carl G. Beatty.
Graphic approach to numerical information processing.
Paper presented at the Eighth Annual Symposium of the Society for Information Display, San Francisco, Calif., May 24-26, 1967, 5 pages.

Graph making has always been a tedious task of coordinating scales, points, and vectors. An experimental program known as GATNIP (Graphic Approach To Numerical Information Processing) uses the computer to transform numerical data into graphs. Numerical information is selectively extracted from existing sequential files and summarized in the form of a graph displayed on the IBM 2250 Display Unit. Automatic scaling and dynamic outline plotting are provided.

A variety of files can be under the control of the program at any given time. Once the file has been chosen, there is considerable leeway as to what data is extracted from the file for plotting. A data range for one or both of the variables involved can be specified. From a simple sequential file, the number of graphs which might be generated from the various combinations is infinite. The program has the capability of displaying multi-plots on the CRT screen. There are 2 references. Abstract by author.

/1967/BEATTY/DJM/computer/interactive/graphics/display/ programs/application/software/.

READER'S COMMENTS -- Interesting presentation, but really essentially a flexible graphical presentation on an IBM 2250 display terminal of already calculated numerical data.

BECK,J 1966.
Jacob Beck.
Effect of orientation and of shape similarity on perceptual grouping.
Perception and Psychophysics 1(1966) 300-302.

A method in which S's were asked to partition a pattern into two regions was used to investigate the perceptual grouping produced by changes in the orientation and shape of two-line figures. The results show that the judged similarity of the figures fails to predict the degree to which the figures form distinct perceptual groups. Grouping was most strongly influenced by differences in the orientation of the lines composing the figures. Crossing of lines making up the figures also affected grouping, but was less decisive than line orientation. There is 1 reference. Abstract by author.

/1966/BECK/perception/psychology/line/pattern/.

READER'S COMMENTS -- There seems to no theoretical or other context for the development of these 2-line figures. It would be hard to build on this research.

BECK,J 1967.
Jacob Beck.
Perceptual grouping produced by line figures.
Perception and Psychophysics 2(1967) 491-495.

Two experiments, one with 2- and one with 3-line figures, studied the relative effectiveness of differences in orientation and shape in producing grouping by similarity. The results showed that changes in shape or orientation which leave the component lines of the figures vertical and horizontal do not facilitate grouping as readily as changes which alter the direction of the component lines to 45 degrees and 135 degrees. These results corroborate and extend the findings of Beck (1966) and are discussed in relation to the problem of specifying the properties of line figures that produce grouping by similarity. There are 6 references. Abstract by author.

/1967/BECK/perception/psycholgy/line/pattern/.

READER'S COMMENTS -- No means are given for the variance analysis.

BECK,P 1967.
Paul Beck
Computer-animated movies
The Vector, Johns Hopkins University (Nov 1967) 17-16.

/1967/BECK/SMZ/computer/animation/.

READER'S COMMENTS -- A brief description of the computer animation process using FORTRAN IV programs and plotting subroutines in comjunction with the SC-4020 is given. The author describes activities at Johns Hopkins under Professor William Huggins and Dr. Doris Entwisle investigating animated movies and the learning process. The paper is a good synopsis of early work at JHU.

BERGER 1970.
S. Berger -- see PALLER 1970.

BERLYNE 1966.
D.E. Berlyne.
Curiosity and exploration.
Science 153(1966) 25-33.

This is a discursive article commenting upon propensity of organisms to seek out novel stimulation. "Novelty" can be taken as irregularity of shape or arrangement, incongruity, amount of heterogeneity of elements. Experiments measuring viewing time attracted by novel stimuli are summarized. Collative variables (ie novelty) are related to information content and are the properties of external stimuli which determine viewing time and like variables. Epistemic curiosity -- seeking out information that will lead to acquisition of knowledge -- is discussed. There are 45 references.

/1966/BERLYNE/DRE/curiosity/novelty/.

BERRY 1968.
J.W. Berry.
Ecology, perceptual development and the Muller-Lyer illusion.
British Journal of Psychology 59(1968) 205-210.

It is generally agreed that any theory of perception must be able to account for illusion and to explain those occasions on which the processing of information results, not in accurate contact with the world, but in systematic distortion. It is not surprising, then, to find that there exist many theoretical attempts to explain illusion, and that, in their haste to find a solution, one theoretical approach typically takes little notice of another.

Two of these theoretical approaches (the "ecological" and the "developmental") have been established at least since the beginning of this century, but only recently (DAWSON 1967) have they been considered in the same work. This report intends to examine these two positions and to show, in some cases, the variables confound one another, yielding insignificant results. However, it will be shown (using Eskimo and

African samples) that, when one class of variables is held constant by appropriate sampling, significant differences in line with both hypotheses do result. There are 24 references. Abstract by author.

/1968/BERRY/DRE/anthropology/perception/illusion/theory/.

BEVAN 1967.
W. Bevan -- see DUKES 1967.

BEVAN 1971.
William Bevan and Joseph A. Steger.
Free recall and abstractness of stimuli.
Science 172(1971)597-599.

This study examines the relation of abstractness of meaningful stimuli to the efficiency of their free recall (actual objects, full-scale black and white photographs of the same objects and printed names of the objects). Abstractness is conceived as a continuum spanning these 3 presentation modes. Ease of recall is inversely related to abstractness of the stimuli. Recall for objects was best, poorer for pictures, poorest for names. For 8 of 9 groups of 4th grade children and for all adults, pictures were superior to words. It is speculated that adult behavior is more versatile than that of the child because the adult, besides his well-developed language skills, has a richer and more thoroughly integrated repertory of multiple cognitive modes. The adults in this experiment clearly were as good as children in the iconic mode, and recalled pictures even better. There are 11 references.

/1971/BEVAN/DRE/seen/abstractness/psychology/iconics/.

BIEDERMAN 1972.
Irving Biederman.
Perceiving real-world scenes.
Science 177(1972)77-79.

When a briefly presented real-world scene was jumbled, the accuracy of identifying a single, cued object was less than that when the scene was coherent. Jumbling remained an effective variable even when the subject knew where to look and what to look for. Thus an object's meaningful context may affect the course of perceptual recognition and not just peripheral scanning or memory. There are 6 references. Abstract by author

/1972/BIEDERMAN/DRE/recognition/picture/structure/.

BIRKHOFF 1943.
George D. Birkhoff.
The mathematical nature of physical theories.
American Scientist 31(1945)281-310.

A master of the difficult and of presenting mathematics in a manner that is intelligible to those in other fields of learning, the author presents his views on the basic relationship between mathematics and physical theories.

/1943/BIRKHOFF/WHH/physical/representation/theory/.

READER'S COMMENTS -- A fascinating article by a great mathematician in which the importance of symmetry and group-theoretical notions in the development of physical theories is emphasized. These ideas have implications for iconics, particularly for portraying physical theory.

BITZER 1968.
D.L. Bitzer and H.G. Slottow.
Principles and applications of the plasma display panel.
1968 Microelectronics and Electronic Systems Symposium, St. Louis, Mo., June 1968, C6-1 -- C6-10.

The Plasma Display Panel stores and displays digital information on an array of gas discharge cells, each of which is isolated from the exciting electrodes. Except when information is changed, every cell is excited by an alternating voltage which, by itself, is insufficient to ignite a discharge. If, however, because of an earlier discharge, there is an accumulation of charge on the insulating end walls, the corresponding wall voltage augments the exciting voltage and a new discharge is ignited. Cells in the "zero" state are characterized by an absence of discharge, and, therefore, an absence of light. Cells in the "one" state are characterized by a sequence of pulse discharges which occur once each half cycle of the exciting voltage. The state of any cell can be changed by the selective application of addressing voltages which, by means of controlled discharges, change the wall charge conditions in the cell.

The technique can be extended to provide variable intensity, and through the use of phosphors, to display information in several colors. The device can be exploited in console displays, in large wall displays; it could form the basis of a new kind of memory, a high speed reproducer of digital information and a high resolution recorder. There are fifteen references. Abstract by author.

/1968/BITZER/SLOTTOW/DJM/computer/graphics/display/hardware/education/.

READER'S COMMENTS -- Relatively inexpensive non-CRT graphics display device. Numerous illustrations describing operation and one showing two characters displayed. Could be made a high resolution display and would be more applicable to character display than vector drawings.

BLOOM 1965.
Burton H. Bloom and Thomas Marill.
CYCLOPS-2: a computer system that learns to see.
Computer Corporation of America, 111 Broadway, Cambridge, Mass. 02142, July 1, 1965.

This project aims to develop a set of interrelated computer techniques to deal with visual recognition, analysis of visual scenes, and learning. The design of CYCLOPS-2 is discussed in detail. At the time of this report it was not complete. When completed, the system will be able to recognize visual shapes composed of arbitrary lines, to analyze scenes composed of such shapes, and to learn (improve its own performance by examining correctly labeled examples). The system of programs include: Input, Preprocessor, Processor, and Output. The entire system has been designed, and the Input, Preprocessor, and part of the Output subsystems have been implemented on the PDP-1 computer. There are no references.

/1965/BLOOM/MARILL/DRE/computer/visual/learning/automatic/system/.

BOGUSLAVSKY 1967.
George W. Boguslavsky.
Study of characteristics contributing to the effectiveness of visual demonstrations.
Final Report Project No. 5-0458, Grant N. 7-42-1070-178, April 1967, Rensselaer Polytechnic Institute, Troy, New York.

Studies were conducted on the instructional merits of visual demonstrations in which details pertinent to the accompanying narrative are highly illuminated, while irrelevant details remain subdued in lesser contrast with the background. Comparisons were made with conventional diagrams in which all details are prominently displayed.

The tests were conducted on high school and college populations in several schools in New York Capital District. The areas of study which served as vehicles for the comparisons were: biology, chemistry, physics, geometry, statistics, and mechanics. Each area was represented by either one or two lectures of about 40 minutes duration.

The results indicate that the experimental slides tend to be somewhat superior to conventional demonstrations in courses requiring illustration of concrete objects, such as biology and mechanics. In courses requiring extensive problem solving, such as chemistry and physics, such superiority was not found, there being some indication of the superiority of the conventional approach. In geometry and statistics the differences, if any, were negligible.

Analysis of effective experimental slides leads to the inference that an effective visual demonstration contains no extraneous details and is capable of commanding attention by selective shifts in figure-ground contrast.

The report questions the assumption that visual demonstrations are necessarily aids and that the closer an illustration resembles the real situation, the greater is its instruction value.

The report refers to Soviet work that casts doubt on both assumptions and points out that a visual demonstration may be a real hindrance if its irrelevant features happen to capture the viewers' attention. In the realistic demonstration the irrelevant features may have prepotency in competing for the viewer's attention.

The main implication of the Soviet research is that a

visual demonstration, to be an aid, must minimize those aspects which are not immediately relevant to the accompanying text. The principle is that of contrast between the feature under discussion and its background.

If the Soviet inferences are correct, the making of instructional visual demonstrations must move in the direction of greater simplicity with attendant reduction in cost. It may also be profitable educationally, as well as financially, to substitute in some phases of teaching schematic outlines of pertinent features for real situations with their concomitant distraction. There are 6 references. Abstract by author.

/1967/BOGUSLAVSKY/education/demonstration/visual/communication/.

BOUKNIGHT 1969.
W.J. Bouknight -- see KADANOFF 1969.

BOWER 1970.
Gordon H. Bower.
Imagery as a relational organizer in associative learning.
Journal of Verbal Learning and Verbal Behavior 9(1970)529-533.

This experiment is designed to clarify how imagery aids learning, whether by increasing cue distinctiveness or by actually improving the association between stimulus and response.

Mental imagery improves paired-associate (PA) learning relative to overt rehearsal. The effect might be due to increased reliability of stimulus encoding or to increased relational association produced by imagery. These hypotheses expect different outcomes when imagery and rote-rehearsal Ss are compared on memory tests of stimulus recognition and on recall of the response term conditional upon stimulus recognition. The Ss learned PAs using one of three methods--rote repetition, interactive imagery, or separation imagery. Associative recall was highest for interactive-imagery Ss and lower and equal for rote- and separation-imagery Ss. No differences in stimulus recognition appeared. Such evidence supports the relational-organizing interpretation of the PA effect of imagery in opposition to the stimulus-distinctiveness or reliable-encoding explanations.

The author suspects that pictures and imagery may be produced by the same relational generating system. This may be a "conceptual deep structure" in which sentences and perceptual experiences are translated for storage and out of which surface sentences, imagery or drawings may be generated, depending on the material and task demands. There are 10 references.

/*PYLYSHYN 1973/.

/1970/BOWER/DRE/psychology/imagery/learning/association/.

READER'S COMMENTS -- From a theoretical viewpoint this is an important paper because it suggests that the effect of imagery on learning comes about by altering the associative process itself.

BROWN,DR 1967.
D.R. Brown and D.H. Owen.
The metrics of visual form: Methodological dyspepsia.
Psychological Bulletin 68(1967)243-59.

A methodological program for the development of a psychophysics of form is outlined with relevant data presented for samples of random polygons. The method emphasizes the importance of viewing form as a multivariate display and the importance of studying the statistical characteristics of the population of shapes from which samples are selected for behavioral studies. Implications for perceptual research are discussed.

/1967/BROWN/OWEN/RAS/perception/shape/pattern/psychology/.

READER'S COMMENTS -- This paper discusses various measures of shape. Statistical charateristics are evaluated so as to provide a uniform population of shapes for perceptual studies. Results have shown that many valid measures are capable of use but research is still needed to find out what measures are significant from the perceptual standpoint.

BROWN,JW 1967.
James W. Brown and James W. Thornton.
Media activity inventory-directory
Mimeo report, San Jose State College, 434 E, William St., San Jose, Calif. 95112.

581 Institutions (out of 652) sent descriptions of new media activities in higher institutions. The inventory is by institution, by person responsible for media activities, and by type of media. There are no references.

/1967/BROWN/DRE/education/media/inventory/.

BRUNER 1966.
Jerome S. Bruner.
Toward a Theory of Instruction.
Cambridge, Mass., Harvard Univ. Press, 1967.

Bruner, with a strong nod in the direction of Piaget's research examines how mental growth proceeds. He looks for ways that teaching can adapt itself to that progression.

Most relevant for iconics is Chapter 1 "Patterns of Growth" which hypothesizes about how the child gets "free of present stimuli and conserves past experience in a model" (p 10). Bruner proposes a three-phase development, with action (enactive), use of summarizing images (iconic), and presentation in words (symbolic) as the phases. Bruner further suggests that intellectual development proceeds through these phases, in the order listed, so a human beng is able to command all three.

By age 3, Bruner states, images develop an autonomous status. Visual memory at this age seems to be highly concrete and specific. He believes some sort of image formation, or sentence formation, comes rather automatically as an accompaniment of response stabilization, but exactly how is not understood. He sees Gestalt theory as the system to use in analyzing the iconic mode.

/*HUGGINS 1968/.

/1967/BRUNER/cognition/memory/education/psychology/.

BRUNSWIK 1953.
E. Brunswik and J. Kamiya.
Ecological cue-validity of "proximity" and of other gestalt factors.
American Journal of Sociology 66(1953)20-32.

Gestalt psychologists have stressed the influence of certain stimulus-factors upon figural unity in perceptual organization. Prominent among these factors are "proximity," "equality" (or "similarity"), "symmetry," "good continuation," and "closure" in the sense of the closedness of a line or pattern in the stimulus-configuration.

According to orthodox Gestalt theory, the effectiveness of these factors rests on dynamic processes inherent in the brain field, rather than on accumulated past experience; while occasioned by respective characteristics of the stimulus-configuration which acts as a set of "topographical" factors at the boundary of the system, the dynamics themselves are in the nature of "physical Gestalten," that is, of a spontaneous physiological "self-distribution" built into the organism prior to, and as a condition for -- rather than as a result of -- learning. For this reason it is also said that the factors mentioned operate in an "autochthonous' manner, that is, are indigenous to the organism so far as their organizational effect is concerned.

A more broadly functionalistic view of perception would suggest an alternative interpretation of the factors of perceptual organization which at the same time would be well in keeping with modern learning theory. According to this view these factors would be seen as guides to the life-relevant physical properties of the remote environmental objects, and thus as playing a part in adjustment; in more technical language, they would be conceived of as proximal.

The possibility of such an interpretation hinges upon the "ecological validity" of these factors, that is, their objective trustworthiness as potential indicators of mechanical or other relatively essential or enduring characteristics of our manipulable surroundings.

The successful demonstration, within any framework stipulated, of the ecological validity of a Gestalt-factor does not automatically imply the legitimacy of its interpretation as a learned cue. It merely shows that an objective basis for probability learning is offered the individual within the framework chosen. Since, however, all ecological validities represent a challenge to the organism for utilization, and since probably many cues are actually being utilized roughly in proportion to the degree of their validity, our findings lend plausibility-support to the reinterpretation of proximity as a cue acquired by generalized probability learning. If this should become possible for other Gestalt factors also, they all could be seen as externally imposed upon, rather than as innately intrinsic to, the processes in the brain; they would then appear as functionally useful rather than as whimsically "autochthonous." It goes without saying that such an interpretation would lose much of its cogency if it would turn out that proximity has similar organizing effects in individuals, groups, or species in whose habitat or culture it has no (or opposite) ecological validity. There are 12 references.

/1953/BRUNSWIK/KAMIYA/DRE/psychology/perception/pattern/ theory/.

BRYDEN 1969.
Joseph E. Bryden.
Design considerations for computer-driven CRT displays.
Computer Design 8(1969)38-46.

Some of the conclusions were as follows. A contrast ratio of at least 2 is required for maximum resolution. Practically, only about four different brightness levels can be used to distinguish data. A flicker-free display would be expected to have a refreshing rate of at least 47 Hz. The line width of characters should be between a tenth and a sixth of the character height. Upper case characters are more legible than lower case ones. The author points out that characters are generated usually in one of three ways: beam shaping, fixed format with appropriate unblanking and cursive or stroke writing. Cursively written characters are favored for high density displays. Sorting of computer addresses according to data groups is recommended for reducing positioning time. Arc drawing line generators and constant-writing speed generators are highly desirable. There are 11 references.

/1969/BRYDEN/DJM/computer/graphics/hardware/design/.

READER'S COMMENTS -- Excellent overview of both human factors and hardware considerations in computer graphic displays.

BUGELSKI 1970.
B.R. Bugelski.
Words and things and images.
American Psychologist 25(1970)1002-1012.

The early history of imagery and its exclusion from 20th century psychology are discussed. Then research on imagery is summarized under 5 major headings:

(1) A basic behavioral approach is to get subjects to use a verbal approach in learning vs an approach forming images. The demonstration that deaf children, with no formal training in language, can learn and remember justifies some reliance on the reality of imagery. Further evidence on the reality of imagery is contained in data on word associations when subjects are asked to respond with "the first thing you think of" (quotes ours) -- about 85 percent of the responses can be classified as images.

(2) Imagery has perhaps also been neglected because it takes time (about 4 to 8 seconds) for a useful image to be formed and verbal materials are customarily presented at a 2-second rate.

(3) Imagery as a mediator has been investigated and imagery, whether supplied by the subject or by the experimenter, aids retention. That supplied by the subject is more effective.

(4) A possible explanation for the effectiveness of imagery involves the absence of interference--images of greater and greater complexity (and uniqueness) can be built.

(5) Meaning seems to depend to a much greater extent on imagery than had been supposed. When M (meaning value) is held constant, learning is strongly dependent on imagery whereas holding imagery constant and letting M vary does not result in a significant relation between M and learning. Words need not arouse the same images, thus precipitating failures in communication. There are 30 references.

/*PYLYSHYN 1973/.

/1970/BUGELSKI/DRE/imagery/meaning/learning/.

BURGER 1968.
John F. Burger -- see SIMMONS 1968.

CAMPBELL 1963.
D.T. Campbell -- see SEGALL 1963.

CAMPBELL 1966.
D.T. Campbell -- see SEGALL 1966.

CARR,CS 1968.
C. Stephen Carr -- see SMITH 1968.

CARR,CS 1969.
C. Stephen Carr.
Geometric modeling.
RADC-TR-69-248, University of Utah, Technical Report June 1969.

A system is presented for modeling three-dimensional objects, such as buildings and mechanical devices, in the computer. The system has been implemented as an interactive design system. Shaded, half-tone photographs of objects designed with the system are included.

An algorithm is presented for quickly determining if two objects, created by the human user, interpenetrate one another. The user is informed of such violations by the system. Additionally, basic concepts of computer graphics modeling are presented for the benefit of readers not conversant with the terminology of computer graphics.

The implementation of these ideas as an interactive design system for architects has been a formidable task on the 1108. A description of this task is included as an appendix. The description should be of interest to systems programmers, however, as the implementation used the most modern programming techniques, such as a compiler/compiler to generate a graphics programming language processor, and a hashed associative data base. There are 12 references. Abstract by author.

/1969/CARR/geometry/interactive/design/spatial/.

CARR,JW 1971.
J.W. Carr -- see TALBOT 1971.

CERMAK 1973.
R.W. Cermak -- see SHEPARD 1973.

CHAPANIS 1967.
Alphonse Chapanis and Donald A. Mankin.
The vertical-horizontal illusion in a visually-rich environment.
Perception and Psychophysics 2(1967)249-255.

In the vertical-horizontal illusion the vertical dimension of a figure typically appears longer than the horizontal. Although there is a large body of research literature on this illusion, all of it refers to simple figures with well-drawn lines, exhibited against plain backgrounds. Our experiment has investigated the illusion using real-world objects in a visually-rich environment. Ten male and 10 female S's were asked to judge the heights of 10 objects of various sizes and shapes. They make their estimates by having the experimenter mark off a horizontal distance that corresponded to the judged height of the object. Each S estimated the height of each object once a day for three consecutive days. The results show that, by and large, the illusion can be demonstrated for real objects in a visually-rich environment. There was, however, considerable variation among the objects. It appears that estimates of this kind may be influenced by size, size constancy, anchor effects, and angle of regard, along with other, and yet, unidentified factors. There are 7 references. Abstract by author.

/1967/CHAPANIS/MANKIN/perception/psychology/illusion/.

CHERNOFF 1971A.
Herman Chernoff.
Faces from numbers make scientists' work easier.
Brief Article from The Stanford Observer (Stanford University News paper), November 1971, page 7.

This news story in the Stanford University Newspaper reports on the use of stylized faces whose features (eyes, mouth, eyebrows, ears, nose and head shape) may be varied in accord with the different components in a numerical N-tuple to provide a quickly recognized representation of these rows of numbers. Slight differences, similarities and groupings in the data often can be seen at a glance in such a series of faces because we are skilled at noting facial characteristics whereas rows of numbers will simply confuse us.

The article shows typical faces used to represent the 12 constituents of geological core samples taken from a Colorado mountain side. The article claims that Chernoff's program will handle up to 18 variables in a single face. There are no references.

/1971/CHERNOFF/WHH/iconic/representation/display/recognition/

READER'S COMMENTS -- A fascinating idea worthy of considerable attention because it uses strong iconic principles.

CHERNOFF 1971B.
Hermann Chernoff.
The use of faces to represent points in n-dimensional space graphically.
Technical Report No. 71, Dept. of Statistics, Stanford University, Stanford, California, December 1971.

A new method of representing multivariate data graphically is described here. Briefly, it consists of representing a point in n-dimensional space by a picture of a face whose characteristics are determined by the position of the point. A sample of points in n-dimensional space is represented by a collection of faces. Two illustrations are sketched briefly. Detailed documentation, including the data for the illustrative examples and the method of generating the faces, is included. Abstract by author. There are 6 references.

/1971/CHERNOFF/RJJ/computer/graphics/communication/applications/software/.

READER'S COMMENTS -- Paper presents an interesting and apparently powerful format for iconic communications. No detailed study of how to use the method or implications of the method appear, though such are certainly warranted.

CHERRY 1969.
Lorinda L. Cherry -- see KNOWLTON,KC 1969B.

CHOMSKY 1958.
N. Chomsky -- see MILLER 1958.

CHUA 1970.
L.O. Chua.
An experiment on the use of computer graphics in teaching of selected topics from nonlinear circuit theory.
Technical Report No. TR-EE 70-43, School of Electrical Engineering, Purdue University, Lafayette, Indiana, December 1970.

This report contains the final documentation for the graphics software and computer programs which have been developed for the area of nonlinear electronic circuits at Purdue University under NSF grant GY5300 to evaluate the merits of computer graphics in undergraduate education. The four software packages consisting of ELIM and COMP, MECA, GAMA and CAPPA are described in complete detail. Part I of this report contains the user's manual for these programs, whereas the complete listings of the above programs are documented in Part II. An evaluation of the usefulness of these programs and student responses is also included.

/1970/CHUA/WHH/computer/graphics/applications/engineering/design/education/software/.

READER'S COMMENTS -- The principal emphasis appears to have been on the development of several powerful and useful programs for dealing with nonlinear circuit behavior. The graphic displays and conventions used are for the most part traditional and appear to have been adopted in a purely ad hoc fashion. The report gives no evidence of an experimental design to evaluate the effectiveness of this apparatus for teaching circuit theory.

CLEMENT 1963.
David E. Clement -- see GARNER 1963.

COONS 1968.
S.A. Coons -- see AHUJA 1968.

CORNWELL 1968.
Bruce Cornwell.
Problem simulation in motion-picture films for intuitive learning.
1968 UAIDE Meeting, San Francisco, California.

COULTER 1971.
R.R. Coulter -- see TALBOT 1971.

DACEY 1962.
Michael F. Dacey and Tze-hsiung Tung.
The identification of randomness in point patterns.
Journal of Regional Science 4(1962).

There are seven references.

/*ROSENFELD 1969/.

/1962/DACEY/TUNG/random/pattern/.

DACEY 1968.
Michael F. Dacey.
The syntax of a triangle and some other figures.
Northwestern University, College of Arts and Sciences, Evanston, Illinois, April 1968.

An approach suggested by Kirsch is used to construct sets of rules for two-dimensional languages that generate arrangements of symbols that form polygons. The syntactic structure of these languages is analyzed and it is shown that a mathematical group summarizes the structure holding between languages constructed for polygons that are related by proper and improper rotations. There are four references. Abstract by author.

/1968/DACEY/language/geometry/.

DAINOFF 1967.
Marvin Dainoff and Ralph N. Haber.
How much help do repeated presentations give to recognition processes.
Perception and Psychophysics 2(1967) 131-136.

A recent experiment by Haber and Hershenson (1965) had shown that in a recognition task one long look at a stimulus was always superior to two or more shorter looks summing to the same total presentation time. In order to explore this more fully and to account for opposite results in a different type of recognition task, as well as in serial learning task, an improved replication of the earlier study was carried out using very short durations and single letters as stimuli. The same non-reciprocity was found, again strongly favoring duration over repetition as a determinant of clarity of a percept, even though repetition alone was also shown to be a significant independent variable. As a subsidiary finding, an error analysis showed that when a letter was misnamed it was nearly always confused with one that looked like it rather than one that sounded like it. Some discussion was offered as to the role of an auditory information storage in low memory load tasks such as this one, as well as some general implications for information processing analyses of the non-reciprocity of duration and repetition. There are 21 references. Abstract by author.

/1967/DAINOFF/HABER/perception/psychology/display/.

DART 1972.
Francis E. Dart.
Science and the worldview.
Physics Today 25(June 1972) 43-54.

This is an interesting discussion of the incompatibility of elementary science concepts with the informal experience of children in other cultures, such as the Nepalese. The suggestion is made that a "prescience" experience should be taught as a "second culture" valid in its own right, in much the same spirit as a second language is taught with no suggestion that one is right and the other is wrong.

Evidence is presented that knowledge "comes from books' and "from old people" for Nepalese informants. In short, knowledge is derived from authority and not from observation.

When asked to draw maps showing how to get "from your house to the school', Nepalese children make sequential maps showing the house and school but are otherwise entirely devoid of spatial structures. In fact, drawing and spatial representations are little used in that culture. These differences must be recognized when presenting science ideas which depend so heavily on spatial structure. There are 4 references.

/1972/DART/WHH/education/physics/children/.

READER'S COMMENTS -- This is one of several articles in a

special issue of Physics Today devoted to science education for children.

DAWSON 1967.
John L.M. Dawson.
Cultural and physiological influences upon spatial-perceptual processes in West Africa--Part I.
International Journal of Psychology 2(1967) 115-128.

DAY 1967.
Hy Day.
Evaluations of subjective complexity, pleasingness and interestingness for a series of random polygons varying in complexity.
Perception and Psychophysics 2(1967) 281-286.

A series of random-shaped polygons varying in number of sides in approximately even logarithmic steps from four to 160 sides was generated. Ss were requries to compare all possible pairs of figures on one of three scales -- subjective complexity, pleasingness and interestingness. Subjective evaluations of complexity continued to increase with informational content. Pleasingness evaluations described a bimodal function, peaking at the 6-sided and 28-sided levels then falling rapidly with increased complexity. Interestingness evaluations rose to a peak at the 28-sided figure and remained high throughout the rest of the series. There are 17 references.

/1967/DAY/perception/psychology/shape/.

DEBES 1970.
John L. Debes -- see WILLIAMS 1970.

DEESE 1965.
James Deese.
The structure of associations in language and thought.
The Johns Hopkins Press, Baltimore, 1965.

DENO 1967.
S.L. Deno -- see JENKINS 1967, JENKINS 1969.

DEREGOWSKI 19681969.
Jan B. Deregowski.
Difficulties in pictorial depth perception in Africa.
British Journal of Psychology 59(1968) 195-204.

Hudson's Pictorial Perception Test and a construction test asking subjects to construct geometrical models shown in pictures were given to Central African schoolboys and domestic servants. The servants had low educational level (3.8 years) but had been exposed to a westernized environment containing magazines and other pictorial materials. The schoolboys had approximately the same amount of education and averaged 12 years in age. The servants averaged 30 years of age. A significant portion of those classed as 2-D perceivers on Hudson's test built 3-D constructions, often distorted or oddly oriented. It appears that passive exposure to material may play only a minor role in pictorial depth perception. There are 11 references.

/1968/DEREGOWSKI/DRE/anthropology/spatial/perception/.

READER'S COMMENTS -- This study calls into doubt findings of earlier studies with Africans showing failure of, or reduction in 3-D perception.

DUKES 1967.
William F. Dukes and William Bevan.
Stimulus variation and repetition in the acquisition of naming responses.
Journal of Experimental Psychology 74(1967 pt. 1) 178-181.

A total of 257 female Ss learned to associate names with photographs, each S serving under 1 of 2 training and test conditions. In one training condition, the same photograph of each person was repeatedly presented; in the other, 4 different photos were used. In one test situation, the test photos were a set that had been used in training; in the other, they were completely new poses. Three different levels of training were used. Results indicated that repetition of particular S-R combinations is the important training principle when the purpose of training is the reinstatement of a particular R to a specific individual S; in contrast, stimulus variation is the significant principle when the purpose is correctly identifying members of a generic class. The significance of these 2 principles was clarified by comparing performance across different levels of training. A general practice effect was also found to be associated with the use of stimulus variation. There are 9 references. Abstract by author.

/1967/DUKES/BEVAN/RJJ/psychology/perception/pattern/recall/category/.

READER'S COMMENTS -- This short paper presents an experiment in the recall of iconic information (bodies and faces) and formation of categories. Results are not interpreted extensively. Several aspects of the research lacked precision; in particular, the similarity or differences between faces was not accurately measurable.

DUNCAN 1969.
Starker Duncan, Jr.
Nonverbal communication.
Psychological Bulletin 72(1969) 118-137.

Certain nonverbal behaviors, such as voice quality (paralanguage), body motion, touch, and use of personal space (proxemics) appear to play a prominent role in communication. Research efforts to specify and to understand the communicative function of these behaviors, here generically termed "nonverbal", are reviewed. A distinction is drawn between two broad research strategies in this area. (A) The structural approach, in which an underlying system or set of rules somewhat analogous to those for language is sought for nonverbal behaviors and (B) the external variable approach, in which statistical relationships are sought between specified nonverbal behaviors and other variables, such as the communication situation, subjects, personality characteristics, other nonverbal behaviors, or judgments of observers. Both structural and external variable studies are surveyed in addition to purely descriptive studies and major transcription systems. There are 100 references. Abstract by author.

/1969/DUNCAN/DRE/psychology/communication/iconic/enactive/.

READER'S COMMENTS -- This article suggests a strategy for research that might also be useful for research in iconic communication, ie research on the underlying system or set of rules needed for iconic communication and research on relations between iconics and other variables, like age.

DWYER 1967.
Francis M. Dwyer, Jr.
Adapting visual illustrations for effective learning.
Harvard Educational Review 37(1967) 250-263.

The author reports his study of the effectiveness of visual illustrations. His findings suggest that increasing amounts of detail in illustrations do not necessarily lead to greater learning. The study raises questions about the meaning of "realism" in visual aids. There are 38 references. Abstract by author.

/1967/DWYER/education/visual/learning/.

DWYER 1970.
Francis M. Dwyer.
Exploratory studies in the effectiveness of visual illustrations.
AV Communication Review 18(1970) 235-249.

A brief review of the literature reveals two opposite views on whether visual aids for education should be realistic or not. Three earlier studies combining four modes of visual presentation with slides, with TV, and with programmed instruction showed little advantage except that realistic photographs seemed most effective with programmed instruction. (There serious differences mar comparisons, such as disparate times spent for various instructional modes.) Later studies showed differences by grade, differences for different subtests within the criterion test, and differences depending on the size of TV images. The author concludes

1. The use of visuals to complement oral and verbal instructions does not automatically improve student achievement.

2. Different visuals differ in the effectiveness with which they promote achievement of learning objectives.

3. The effectiveness of specifications of visual material depends on the method used to present this material to the student.

4. For students in different grade levels, the same

visuals are not equally effective in increasing student achievement of identical objectives.

5. For specific objectives the addition of color in certain types of visuals, for students in specific grade levels, appears to be an important instructional variable in improving student achievement.

6. The effectiveness of particular visual in facilitating student achievement of a specific objective depends on the type of information needed by the student to achieve that objective..

/1970/DWYER/DRE/education/visual/color/effectiveness/.

EGETH 1971.
Howard Egeth, John Jonides and Sally Wall.
Unlimited-capacity parallel processing of multielement displays.
Unpublished paper, The Johns Hopkins University.

The spatiotemporal characteristics of mechanisms that extract information from complex alphanumeric displays were investigated in three experiments using search and same-different tasks. The number of randomly arranged stimulus elements was the major independent variable and reaction time was the dependent variable. Overall the data suggest that an unlimited capacity parallel model with fixed-interval sampling may be able to account for performance in these experiments. However, it is possible that a serial model may be applicable to the conditions of low discriminability. There are 13 references. Abstract by author.

/1971/EGETH/JONIDES/WALL/RAS/perception/psychology/visual/model/.

READER'S COMMENTS -- This is an interesting research paper on the methods of perception comparing serial processing to parallel processing of arrays of symbols.

EGETH 1972.
Howard Egeth, John Jonides, and Sally Wall.
Parallel processing of multi-element displays.
Cognitive Psychology 3(1972)674-698.

The spatiotemporal characteristics of mechanisms that extract information from complex alphanumeric displays are investigated in a series of experiments using search and "same-different" detection tasks. Under several (but not all) experimental conditions the functions relating reaction time to the numbers of elements in the display were flat. Such data are consistent with a model in which individual elements are examined by independent parallel channels. Interestingly, this model was appropriate even in a search task in which the target was specified as any digit and the non-targets were a random assortment of letters. Abstract by author. 32 references.

/*EGETH 1973/.

/1972/EGETH/JONIDES/WALL/WHH/psychology/visual/display/symbol/recognition/.

READER'S COMMENTS -- When asked to decide if "all elements of the display are the same," subjects responded more slowly than when asked if "any element is different," even though the questions are logically equivalent (since one implies the negation of the other). This suggests that the examination of the display proceeds differently for the two ways of posing the question.

EGETH 1973.
Howard Egeth, Janette Atkinson, Grover Gilmore, and Norman Marcus.
Factors affecting processing mode in visual search.
Perception and Psychophysics 13(1973)394-402.

Visual search was studied under a variety of conditions to clarify some differences among the results of previous investigations and to provide a testing grounds for models of visual information processing. Display configuration, target and field composition, exposure duration, and display size (up to 16 elements) were among the parameters investigated. In some conditions, mean reaction time was essentially invariant with display size, while in other conditions it increased substantially and linearly with display size. Current models of visual information processing were evaluated in the light of these and previous findings: all were found wanting. The data seem to demand a system subject to flexible cognitive control processes. Abstract by author. There are 24 references.

/1973/EGETH/ATKINSON/GILMORE/MARCUS/WHH/psychology/display/symbol/recognition/.

READER'S COMMENTS -- Paper reports evidence that "mental set" radically alters reaction time. For instance, when the character "O" in a set of other alphabetical characters is referred to as the letter "O", subjects perform differently than when the same character is referred to as the numeral "O".

ENGVOLD 1968.
K.J. Engvold and J.L. Hughes.
A general-purpose display processing and tutorial system.
Communications of the ACM 11(1968)697-702.

ADEPT(A Display Expedited Processing and Tutorial) system is described. This system was designed to improve man-computer communications by employing a display unit to interleave tutoring with other computer operations such as simulation, programming, and information retrieval. It is written in Fortran IV (G) for the IBM System/360, Model 40, and the IBM 2250 Display Unit under Operating System/360. ADEPT is a cataloged program that controls the standard operating system by terminating and rescheduling itself automatically, relinquishing computer resources allocated to it, and surrendering control to the operating system to perform other jobs. It expands the power and flexibility of computer-assisted instruction by making immediately available to students, teachers, and other users, the full resources (system-cataloged programs) of the operating system.

Language processors and compilers, simulation models, mathematical solution techniques, stored data, and all other library and user programs can be incorporated into instructional material without reprogramming. Illustrations of the various applications are presented and their implications are discussed. There are six references. Abstract by authors.

/1968/ENGVOLD/HUGHES/DJM/education/computer/education/system/program/simulation/graphics/.

READER'S COMMENTS -- potentially very useful if graphics to include software developed for other purposes. Many good illustrations on how the system works.

ENTWISLE 1968.
Doris R. Entwisle -- see HUGGINS 1968.

ENTWISLE 1973A.
Doris R. Entwisle and W.H. Huggins.
Iconic memory in children.
Child Development 44(1973) 392-394.

Data on the development of iconic memory in children are reported. Informal observation of nursery school children indicates they can recognize complicated visual materials after short exposure and distinguish them from materials not seen. In an experiment with first-grade children, forty slides of landscapes or cityscapes were shown in rapid succession. Later these slides of unremarkable scenes, all unfamiliar to the children, were recognized with surprising accuracy after periods of time varying from a few hours to one week. Further observations of second-grade children suggest that children are considerably less proficient in recognizing verbal materials describing the scenes depicted in the slides. The long retention of information presented visually to young children is surprising and needs more exploration. There are 3 references. Abstract by the author.

/1973/ENTWISLE/HUGGINS/DRE/perception/psychology/development/.

ENTWISLE 1973B.
Doris R. Entwisle -- see FEINMAN 1973.

ERDAHL 1969.
Alan C. Erdahl.
Displaying computer generated half-tone pictures in real time.
RADC-TR-69-250 Technical Report, June 1969, Rome Air Development Center. New York.

The paper describes a system which will allow computer generated half-tone pictures to be displayed in real time.

Half-tone or shaded pictures are valuable since they allow object surfaces to be displayed.

The picture must first be described in terms of its visible surface boundaries. This is a convenient form since the information required is produced by the hidden line algorithms used to generate the picture. Such a form usually represents a substantial savings in the number of bits required to describe a picture.

A display generator is described which will convert these edge descriptions into intensity values which can then be displayed on a raster scan device. A 512 by 512 point picture can be generated in less than 1/30 of a second. This picture can then be displayed directly on an oscilloscope or placed on a storage disk which will refresh a standard television set. There are 5 references. Abstract by author.

/1969/ERDAHL/DJM/computer/graphics/communication/halftone/display/system/.

EVANS 1964.
Thomas G. Evans.
A heuristic program to solve geometric-analogy problems.
Proceedings, Spring Joint Computer Conference 24(1964)327-338. See also Ph.D. Thesis, Dept of Mathematics, Mass. Inst. of Technology, June, 1963.

The purpose of this paper is to describe a LISP program calld ANALOGY which is capable of solving a wide class of the so-called "geometric-analogy" problems frequently encountered on intelligence tests. Each member of this class of problems consists of a set of labeled line drawings. The task to be performed can be concisely described by the question: "figure A is to figure B as figure C is to which of the given figures?" There are 17 references. Abstract by author.

/1964/EVANS/JAB/analogy/representation/association/artificial/intelligence/geometric/program/.

READER'S COMMENTS -- Good example of a computer's ability to work with iconic symbols.

FEDER 1968.
Jerome Feder.
Language of encoded line patterns.
Information and Control 13(Sept 1968)230-244.

By treating patterns as statements in a two-dimensional language, it is possible to apply linguistic theory to pattern analysis and recognition. In this paper, line patterns are encoded into string form using the chain code developed by Freeman. A class of patterns, or pattern language, encodes to a set of strings that is examined using theory that exists for string languages and automata. Pattern languages formed on the basis of equations in two variables and various pattern properties are related to the hierarchy of string language classes. The known relationships between classes of string languages and classes of automata can then be applied to determine bounds on the time and memory required to recognize the various patterns. Results can be extended to other forms of pattern encoding provided that a suitable translator can be constructed. There are 15 references. Abstract by author.

/1968/FEDER/TWB/linguistics/pattern/language/.

READER'S COMMENTS -- Very theoretical and requires learning author's notation.

FEDER 1969.
Jerome Feder.
Linguistic specification and analysis of classes of line patterns.
Technical Report 403-2, New York University, April 1969.

When attempting to recognize or structurally analyze patterns it is useful to consider the patterns as being statements in a two-dimensional language. In the first part of this thesis, geometric curves are encoded into string form using the chain code developed by Freeman. A class of patterns, or pattern language, encodes to a set of strings that is analyzed using the large body of theory that exists for string languages. Pattern languages formed on the basis of equations in two variables, pattern properties and various notations of similarity to an arbitrary given curve are related to the hierarchy of string language classes. The known relationships between classes of string languages and classes of automata can then be applied to determine bounds on the time and memory required to recognize the various curves. The extension of results to other pattern encoding schemes is considered.

In the second part of the thesis the grammar scheme used for defining string languages is extended to structures composed of entities with N**2 "attaching points". By means of the more general grammar, it is possible to specify the combination and interconnection of geometric curves and thus extend the results of the first part of the thesis to treat pattern classes containing mesh-like line patterns. The new grammar is of additional interest in that many important classes of structures can be linguistically specified and studied; chemical structure diagrams, circuit diagrams, logic diagrams and computer flow charts are interconnections of entities with N attaching points.

An algorithm for parsing a "context-free" structure language according to its grammar specification is given. This algorithm is applied to structures obtained from line patterns to obtain a table-driven pattern analyzer. This device is an extension to two dimensions of a universal or table-driven compiler and is able to perform a broad range of pattern analysis tasks on widely differing classes of patterns. The table-driven pattern analyzer is applied to detecting events in bubble-chamber photographs. A particular advantage of the device is that the event being searched for can be changed by simply changing the entries in program tables containing the syntax of the event, although the current version of the table-driven pattern analyzer accepts patterns and structures furnished in other ways. There are 50 references. Abstract by author.

/1969/FEDER/DJM/computer/picture/language/pattern/.

FEINMAN 1973.
Saul Feinman and Doris R. Entwisle.
Person perception according to race.
Paper presented at 22nd Annual Research Institute of the District of Columbia Sociological Society, Washington, D.C., 1973 (Mimeo., Johns Hopkins University).

A study of 1st, 2nd, 3rd and 6th grade children was carried out with children identifying a set of 20 target pictures. The target pictures contain 10 blacks, 10 whites, with equal numbers of the two sexes. Results were that members of the same race are better recognized (whites are better at recognizing white faces). The scores increase rapidly with age up to third grade and level off thereafter. A small sample of college undergraduates obtained recognition scores of about the same level as third graders. There are 4 references. Abstract by the author.

/1973/FEINMAN/ENTWISLE/DRE/perception/development/psychology/.

FELTS 1971.
Wayne Felts -- see KROLAK 1971.

FIRSCHEIN 1970.
O. Firschein and M.A. Fischler.
Describing and abstracting pictorial structures.
Information Sciences Laboratory LMSC 6-80-70-37A, November, 1970.

The concept of a pictorial data base consisting of descriptions of pictures is introduced; the nature and problems of the descriptive process is discussed. Most discussion is in the form of quotations from the 45 cited references.

Three main classes of formal descriptive technique are examined:

I. The grammar-based approach which uses a set of rules or productions to create a phrase structure grammar which can describe the arrangement and relationship of graphic primitives.

II. The descriptor-based approach which attempts to reveal the content of the picture by using a number of terms or phrases. This approach is generally used for retrieval.

III. The procedure-based approach which uses high-level intervention by man to create a desired description where many descriptions can be generated. This approach allows much naturalness and semantic capability, although none of the approaches deals successfully with grey-level pictures. There are 45 references. Abstract by author.

/1970/FIRSCHEIN/FISCHLER/BLC/pictures/grammars/retrieval/procedures/primitives/.

READER'S COMMENTS -- A useful survey of existing literature on the topic of generating and retrieving formal descriptions of pictorial data, both static and dynamic.

FISCHLER 1969.
Martin A. Fischler.
Machine perception and description of pictorial data.
California, Lockheed Palo Alto Research Laboratory, March 1969.

This investigation of machine processing of pictorial data is based on the premise that people can recognize visual objects and describe them well enough so that other individuals can recognize the objects from the description. Given a system of linguistic communication between a person and a digital computer, and given that the computer possesses adequate perceptual machinery, many currently refractory problems in pictorial data processing would be open to solution.

This paper describes a computer system which can perceive a limited class of graphical objects, create linguistic descriptions for the objects, and classify objects by comparison with a reference set of descriptions as might be produced in normal human communication. There are 22 references. Abstract by author.

/1969/FISCHLER/DGW/computer/perception/representation/communication/.

READER'S COMMENTS -- This paper describes some computer programs that are basically curve following routines. The program produces a linguistic description of the curves that are traced. Without a listing of the programs and sufficient examples showing their operation on real problems, it is impossible to evaluate the author's claims.

FISCHLER 1970.
Martin A. Fischler -- see FIRSCHEIN 1970.

FORGIE 1969.
James W. Forgie -- see SUTHERLAND,WR 1969.

FORSDALE 1970.
Joan R. Forsdale and Louis Forsdale.
Film literacy.
AV Communication Review 18(1970)263-276.

The major thrust of the article is toward documenting the need for instruction and training in film viewing. A rich set of examples, drawn from reports of primitive peoples, suggest a ladder of film literacy (1) total non-comprehension, (2) comprehension of separate objects, (3) confusion of picture with reality, (4) no understanding of the simplest film conventions, (5) incomprehension of, or indifference to, the unfamiliarity. A plea is made for giving instruction in film-viewing as a basic educational topic. There are 16 references.

/1970/FORSDALE/DRE/literacy/cinema/education/.

FOY 1964.
Wade H. Foy, Jr.
Entropy of simple line drawings.
IEEE Transactions on Information Theory 10(1964) 165-167.
/1964/FOY/SMA/communication/data/line/theory/.

READER'S COMMENTS -- As an attack on the problem of communication of simple line drawings over a transmission link, the entropy of a general class of line drawings is computed. This statistic is of use in setting a lower bound on the channel capacity required in the transmission medium.

The article is of peripheral interest to iconic communications, relating more to the technical problems of information transmission.

FREEMAN 1968.
R. B. Freeman -- see KILBRIDE 1968.

FRISCH 1966.
H.L. Frisch and B. Julesz.
Figure-ground perception and random geometry.
Perception and Psychophysics 1(1966) 389-398.

Constructs of random geometry were applied to the problem of figure-ground perception. Random dot images of black and white dots with various area fractions and tesselations (square and triangular lattices) were used as stimuli. The constructs of random geometry are correlation functions of N-th order and some functionals defined on them. The only parameter which is independent of tesselation used is the first-order correlation which is the area fraction. It was first conjectured and then experimentally verified that figure-ground perception is not affected by the various tesselations used. Thus, figure-ground phenomena depend only on the area fraction of the white and black dots in the stimulus. There is a perceptual bias for white, that is, figure-ground reversal is easiest at 40 percent white-black area fraction. It was also experimentally shown that size-constancy prevails in figure-ground perception, but brightness-constancy does not. There are 12 references. Abstract by author.

/1966/FRISCH/JULEZ/JWW/psychology/perception/model/.

READER'S COMMENTS -- Authors construct probabilistic models designed to test for ambiguity in figure-ground reversals in perception. Random geometry generated by the computer is used to test the hypotheses proposed. Evaluation of data by analysis of variance. Frisch and Julesz have tried to quantify an aspect of perception.

GALTON 1883.
F. Galton.
Inquiries into Human Faculty and its Development.
Macmillan, New York, 1883.

The first definitive inquiry using a questionnaire and the first statistical survey into the use of imagery by men of science. Galton concluded that "scientific men, as a class, have feeble powers of visual representation." He attributes this to the liklihood that "an over-ready perception of sharp mental pictures is antagonistic to the acquirement of habits of highly generalized and abstract thought, especially when the steps of reasoning are carried on by words as symbols, and that if the faculty of seeing the pictures was ever possessed by men who think hard, it is very apt to be lost by disuse. The highest minds are probably those in which it is not lost, but subordinated, and is ready for use on suitable occasions."

Galton pleads eloquently for the further development and utilization of visual imagery: "There can, however, be no doubt as the the utility of the visualizing faculty when it is duly subordinated to the higher intellectual operations. A visual image is the most perfect form of mental representation whenever the shape, position, and relations of objects in space are concerned....Our bookish and wordy education tends to repress this valuable gift of nature. A faculty that is of importance in all technical and artistic occupations, that gives accuracy to our perceptions, and justness to our generalizations, is starved by lazy disuse, instead of being cultivated judiciously in such a way as will on the whole bring the best return. I believe that a serious study of the best method of developing and utilizing this faculty, without prejudice to the practice of abstract thought in symbols, is one of the many pressing desiderata in the yet unformed science of education."

/*ROE 1951/*ARNHEIM 1971/.

/1883/GALTON/WHH/psychology/.

READER'S COMMENTS -- The above quotation seems to be an apt description of Einstein (see HOLTON 1971).

GARNER 1963.
Wendell R. Garner and David E. Clement.
Goodness of patterns and pattern uncertainty.
Journal of Verbal Learning and Verbal Behavior 2(1963)446-452.

GARNER 1966.
Wendell R. Garner -- see HANDEL 1966.

GARNER 1970.
Wendell R. Garner.
Good patterns have few alternatives.
American Scientist 58(1970)34-42.

This paper reports a psychophysical experiment where 5 dots are distributed on a 3 X 3 grid with the restriction that no row or column of the grid be empty. This yields 90 possible arrangements. Subjects then viewed these 90 dot patterns and rated them on a 7-point scale from "good" to "poor." Two patterns are invariant under a set of 8 transformations (rotations, reflections). These are highly redundant. Other patterns are medium or low redundant. Garner's experimental data support the hypothesis that patterns with few alternatives when transformed (highly redundant) are preferred by subjects. There are 7 references.

/1970/GARNER/DRE/psychology/visual/pattern/structure/.

READER'S COMMENTS -- This paper is very important because it proposes a measure that can be applied to characterize "goodness of pattern." The measure also suggests a "theory" for human processing of iconic data.

GIBSON,EJ 1970.
Eleanor J. Gibson.
The development of perception as an adaptive process.
American Scientist 58(1970)98-107.

Perception is defined as abstracting information from stimulation; a highly adaptive process. Animals learn to perceive by extracting invariant information from the variable flux. Several attentional processes are involved: perceptual abstraction, the filtering of the irrelevant, active exploratory search. Termination of search comes about by internal reinforcement, the reduction of uncertainty. The search for invariants is the task of perception, and detection of them reduces uncertainty and is reinforcing.

Two modes of perception are (1) Space and events in space, and (2) Objects and permanent items. Monitoring of events in space seems to develop earlier and be more primitive than fine-grain identification of objects like letters (ambient vision vs focal vision). Responses to magnification, avoidance of a falling-off place, and perceived constancy appear very early and are examples of the first type of perception. There is a short course of learning and great continuity over species. Fine-grain differentiation of multidimensional sets of objects is high in the evolutionary scale and in development, and the process is achieved only through education. There are 33 references.

/1970/GIBSON,EJ/DRE/psychology/perception/adaptive/abstraction.

READER'S COMMENTS -- This excellent article clearly delineates two areas of visual perception. It has great relevance for iconics.

GIBSON,JJ 1950.
James J. Gibson.
The Perception of the Visual World.
Boston: Houghton Mifflin Company, 1950.

There are 121 references. No abstract.

/*HOLTON 1965/*HOLT 1964/*KOLERS 1968/*ROBERTS 1963/.

/1950/GIBSON,JJ/perception/psychology/visual/.

READER'S COMMENTS -- A older book of major importance that is still timely in its observations.

GILMORE 1973.
Grover Gilmore -- see EGETH 1973.

GOLDBERG 1951.
Herman D. Goldberg.
The role of "cutting" in the perception of the motion picture.
Journal of Applied Psychology 35(1951)70-71.

The concept formed by the perception of a motion picture is shown to be more dependent upon the sequences as a whole than the reaction to individual scenes which have been spliced together. S's viewed identical scenes set in different contexts and perceived significantly different emotions. Significant also was the order in which the two films were viewed. There are 4 references. Abstract by author.

/1951/GOLDBERG/BLC/film/perception/cutting/.

GOLDSTEIN 1971.
Jay Goldstein, Leon D. Harmon, and Ann B. Lesk.
Identification of human faces.
Proceedings of the IEEE 59(1971)748-760.

How well can human faces be identified by humans and by computers, using subjectively judged "feature" descriptions like long ears, wide-set eyes, etc? Three classes of experiments are reported, (1) Gathering, analysis, and assessment of face-feature data for 255 faces. (2) Computer identification-studies. (3) Human identification-studies. A set of 22 features was evolved from an initially larger set to provide relevant, distinctive, relatively independent measures which can be judged reliably. Computer studies and a mathematical model established limits of performance of a person attempting to isolate a face from a population using feature descriptions. The model predicts that under certain conditions approximately 6 of an individual's features are required to isolate him from a population of 255. Human experiments under similar conditions showed unique identification occurred with an average of about 7 features. The model predicts that for a population of 4 X 10**6, only 14 feature-descriptions are required. These studies form a foundation for continuing research on real-time man-machine interaction for computer classification and identification of multidimensional vectors specified by noisy components. There are 5 references. Abstract by author.

/1971/GOLDSTEIN/DRE/psychology/perception/person perception/.

READER'S COMMENTS -- The specification of this problem is important for social psychological applications (person perception) but also in terms of more general human ability to process and store complex visual information.

GOLDSTEIN 1972.
A.J. Goldstein, L.D. Harmon and A.B. Lesk.
Man-machine interaction in human-face identification.
Bell System Technical Journal 51(1972)399-428.

The objective is to explore new techniques for obtaining accurate recognition of vectors (faces with 21 features rated) given imprecise component values. (This paper is closely related to GOLDSTEIN 1971.) The problem is to find the best match between an unidentified individual and a member of a file population.

In these experiments a subject is shown a picture and asked to describe it to a computer using features from a list given him. The computer then searches for the best-fitting description. The aims of this study include A) developing a decision-making technique using rank-ordering of a population according to some goodness-of-fit criterion, B) designing algorithms to take advantage of strong points of humans and computers, and C) devising a performance measure.

In the interactive system at each step the computer can select the feature which is most likely to be discriminating, and population members are ranked by weights reflecting the match between the portrait description and actual value. Even in the worst case there is fair performance in singling out a target and narrowing down the population. In the best case population reduction is excellent. The target was in first place by portrait's end 67% of the time. There are 5 references.

/1972/GOLDSTEIN/HARMON/LESK/DRE/computer/recognition/face/.

GOMBRICH 1969.
E.H. Gombrich.
Art and Illusion.
Bollingen Paperback, Princeton: Princeton University Press, third printing, 1969.

This brilliant book is based on the A.W. Mellon Lectures in the Fine Arts given at the National Gallery of Art in 1956. It is a scholarly book that almost immediately became a best seller--and for good reason. It is directed to those who seek a meeting ground between science and the humanities. Professor Gombrich uses modern themes of visual perception, information, and learning to scrutinize the history and psychology of pictorial representation. In seeking to explain changing styles of art, he is led to reexamine many current ideas on the imitation of nature, the function of tradition, and other problems. To test his arguments, he ranges wide over the history of art, noticing particularly the accomplishments of those inventors of artistic illusion, the ancient Greeks, and the visual discoveries of such masters as Leonardo da Vinci and Rembrandt, as well as the impressionists and cubists. Yet his main concern is with ourselves, the beholders, and he includes an analysis of humbler pictorial documents and the inventions of humorists and commercial artists.

The text contains over 300 illustrations in half-tone and line, of which 18 are in color. There are 41 pages of notes and a detailed index.

/1969/GOMBRICH/WHH/art/visual/representation/.

GREEN,BF 1961.
Bert F. Green, Jr.
Figure coherence in the kinetic depth effect.
Journal of Experimental Psychology 62(1961)272-282.

Six experiments examined the extent to which the kinetic depth effect produces perceived coherence and rigidity of random figures. Subjectively rated coherence was greater with (A) More elements in the figure, (B) Connections and constraints among the elements, and (C) Less complex axes of rotation. The tumbling rotation was shown to be intermediate between simple and complex axes of spinning rotations. Speed of rotation was shown to have almost no effect. Individual differences were large. A high speed digital computer was essential for producing the stimuli for the experiments. There are 7 references. Abstract by author.

/1961/GREEN/perception/psychology/spatial/movement/illusion/.

GREEN,RE 1969,1971.
R. Elliot Green -- see PARSLOW 1969,1971.

GRENANDER 1969.
Ulf Grenander.
A unified approach to pattern analysis.
Brown University Center for Computer and Information Sciences and Division of Applied Mathematics, 1969.

This paper approaches the problem of pattern analysis from a formal and theoretical point of view. The author first defines seven criteria for a formal approach to pattern analysis. He then suggests a mathematics for implementing these criteria. Several examples are given to show how the formalisms look in concrete situations. For anyone considering serious work in pattern analysis this paper is of definite value. The introduction is recommended to anyone faced with the problem of organizing new material. There are 14 references.

/1969/GRENANDER/DGW/mathematics/pattern/theory/.

GROPPER 1968.
G.L. Gropper.
Programming visual presentations for procedural learning.
AV Communication Review 16(1968)33-56.

Television tapes (4) of the assembly of a 3-pole elcetric motor were prepared. Instruction in both recognition and actual assembly of the motor was the goal of instruction. The tapes allowed practice at different times and of different types. Problems and checklists accompanied the lesson. Errors in performance increased as the size of the demonstration unit increased. Actual practice in assembly was more effective in reducing errors than recognition practice.

The techniques used in this study resemble those used in programmed instruction.

This study is an example of a careful empirical investigation of the effectiveness of tapes to teach specific skills. Behavioral indices (assembly performance errors) are used. There are 14 references.

/1968/GROPPER/DRE/education/visual/learning/.

READER'S COMMENTS -- This study suggests a paradigm for empirical investigation of iconic communication -- if performance measures are used, the effectiveness of communication can be assessed without the mediation of verbal symbols.

GYR 1966.

J.W. Gyr, J.S. Brown, R. Willey, and A. Zirvian.
Computer simulation and psychological theories of perception.
Psychological Bulletin 65(1966) 174-192.

Theories of perception which regard the perceiver as active are reviewed: Gibson (percepts are higher order variables discovered by the perceiver); Hebb (emphasizing phenomena of selection as well as attention in perception); Sperry (perception depends on complex integrations involving cortical areas in addition to the visual island); Kohler (invariants are noted between processes in the visual pathway and motor processes employed by the active perceiver in attaining perceptual inputs); von Holst (organisms accept or do not accept a given input as stimulus for further action depending upon relations recorded between self and the environment); Held (at least certain perceptual invariants are connected with the internal "motor language" of the organism); and others.

What can be concluded about the differences between active and passive perception? (1) There may be differences in the dimensions of environmental input which are abstracted as invariant. (2) A given percept may depend on efferent as well as afferent processes -- for the motoric may determine what flux of sensory events comes into the retina next.

The implications of these speculations for computer simulation of perceptual processes are then discussed. There are 50 references.

/1966/GYR/DRE/perception/psychology/computer/simulation/ theory/.

READER'S COMMENTS -- In reviewing the psychological basis for computer work in pattern perception, these authors emphasize those aspects of pattern perception most relevant for iconics.

HABER 1967.

Ralph N. Haber 1967 -- see AINOFF 1967.

HABER 1969A.
Ralph N. Haber.
Eidetic images.
Scientific American 220(1969) 36-44.

Twenty eidetic children (out of 500 tested) were found. The eidetic ability bears no relation to other characteristics of the child but is itself highly reliable. Three to 5 seconds is needed to produce an image. Naming an image apparently destroys the image. Duration of the image is highly variable, from one to ten minutes. The author is not able to determine how much information an eidetic image can contain. Several kinds of evidence (pp. 43-44) suggest that images are visual in nature and do not depend on memory in any way. A further test, involving fusion of 2 separate pictures, is being developed. There are 14 references.

/1969/HABER/DRE/psychology/visual/images/cognition/.

HABER 1969B.
Ralph N. Haber.
How we remember what we see.
Scientific American 220(1969) 104-112.

In an experiment with adults subjects were able to recognize as many as 600 pictures they had seen for only a short period of time. In another test subjects were shown 2560 slides at the rate of one every 10 seconds. One hour later a subject was shown 280 pairs of pictures. One member of each pair was from the set shown previously. Answers were from 85% to 95% correct. Subjects with massed viewing did as well as more leisured viewers. There are no references.

/1969/HABER/DRE/psychology/perception/linguistic/memory/images/cognition/.

READER'S COMMENTS -- This paper is highly relevant to problems in iconic communication and to an understanding of the basic nature of iconic communication. The evidence that there is almost an unlimited capacity for memory of pictures points to a great under-utilization of iconics in education.

HALE 1970.
Gordon A. Hale.
Interrelations in children's learning of verbal and pictorial paired associates.
Paper presented at meetings of American Educational Research Association, Minneapolis, March, 1970.

The author proposes two explanations for why pictures are easier to learn than words (1) Pictorial and verbal associations are learned by essentially different means, (2) Both are learned by verbal association but pictorial representation serves as an additional aid to learning. To get some basis for choosing between these hypotheses, third, sixth and ninth grade children did paired associates tasks using different types of materials (1) Concrete words, (2) Abstract words, (3) Pictures that were line drawings of the concrete words, (4) 5-stroke Japanese characters (abstract line drawings). Stimulus elements were nonsense trigrams of high association value. Pictorial presentation of materials was generally more effective than verbal, and there appeared to be a developmental increase in the effectiveness of the pictorial mode. The experiment does not provide unequivocal data with respect to the two hypotheses noted at the outset. There are 8 references.

/1970/HALE/DRE/imagery/learning/psychology/.

READER'S COMMENTS -- The same child who saw concrete words and associated them with trigrams saw pictures of the concrete words and associated them with different trigrams. This seems a serious error in design.

HAMMOND 1971.
Kenneth R. Hammond.
Computer graphics as an aid to learning.
Science 172(1971)903-908.

The paper points to the lack of teaching tools in the area of multiple-cue probability learning (diagnosis is an example). In complex judgmental tasks, outcome feedback and much repetition are required to validate judgments and yet may bear little relation to the process of making judgments themselves. Also getting experts to verbalize their process of judgment may not be helpful because the expert is frequently unaware of, or misinterprets, his own cognitive acts.

In a learning task constructed to simulate a diagnostic problem, a subject was required to integrate information provided by 3 cues where the cues are non-linear and differentially related to the criterion. Five groups of subjects were run: outcome only, outcome plus cue weights (graphic), outcome plus function (graphic), outcome plus cue weights plus function (verbal), and outcome plus cue weights plus function (graphic). The last three groups did learn to apply their knowledge but learning was slow and inefficient and never did reach the statistical limits of achievement. In a further study, properties of the judgmental system and properties of the task were made available on a CDC 282 visual interactive display console. When graphical displays showing the subject's cue-weighting system and the functional relations between his judgment and each cue are used to aid learning, learning is rapid. The display enabled the learner to see quickly what he was expected to do and what he actually did. The potential of this strategy for education is pointed out, especially for cases where there is little chance to develop skill in the application of knowledge (medical schools in Latin American countries). There are 15 references.

/1971/HAMMOND/DRE/interactive/graphics/education/cognitive/training/.

READER'S COMMENTS -- This application of computer graphics

has merit since no other method of presentation seems to offer either rapidly enough or intelligibly enough the feedback by which the learner can judge his performance.

HANDEL 1966.
Stephen Handel and Wendell R. Garner.
The structure of visual pattern associates and pattern goodness.
Perception and Psychophysics 1(1966) 33-38.

Two tasks were used with a total set of 126 dot patterns. In one task Ss rated the goodness of each pattern. In another task they produced a dot pattern as an associate to each of the patterns used as a stimulus. The distributions of the associates suggest that the total set of patterns is both partitioned and nested. Groups defined by rotation and reflection are partitioned, thus kept intact. These groups in turn form a series of nested subsets. Both partitioning and nesting produce subsets of different size. The size of these subsets is related to pattern goodness, with good patterns coming from small subsets. There are 4 references. Abstract by author.

/1966/HANDEL/GARNER/perception/psychology/visual/pattern/.

HARMON 1969.
Leon D. Harmon and Kenneth C. Knowlton.
Picture processing by computer.
Science 164(1969) 19-29.

Some real-world picture, typically a 35 mm transparency, is scanned by a machine like a television camera. The resultant electrical signals, representing the brightness of the successive picture elements, are changed by an A-to-D converter into numerical representations on magnetic tape. This provides a digital version of the input picture for computer processing. A general purpose computer is programmed to process the picture according to algorithms. Then the output is processed to provide a photographic end-product. Several kinds of transformations are possible: picture-to-picture, picture-to-abstraction, data-to-picture, abstraction-to-picture. The new technology makes it possible for one to "see" the invisible, enhances the exercise of the imagination, and permits experiments to be done with a flexibility and rapidity that otherwise would make those experiemnts prohibitive or impossible. There are 51 references.

/1969/HARMON/KNOWLTON/DRE/computer/picture/transformation/.

HARMON 1971A.
Leon D. Harmon.
Some aspects of recognition of human faces.
Pp 196-219 in Pattern Recognition in Biological and Technical Systems, New York: Springer-Verlag, 1971.

Automatic recognition of human faces has rarely been explored, similarly, human ability to recognize faces has received little formal attention. This paper reports some preliminary steps to examine both. Three separate studies are described: (1) Two sets of artist's drawings, one made from literal descriptions, the other made from photographs, are used in human recognition and preference tests; (2) Precisely blurred computer-processed portraits are used in human recognition experiments; (3) Face-feature descriptor sets are tested both for human and for computer classification of faces. In each study the level of performance exceeds informal a priori expectations. There are 12 references. Abstract by author.

/1971/HARMON/RJJ/pattern/recognition/information/encoding/faces/graphics/.

READER'S COMMENTS -- The paper is something of a potpourri of findings related only by their bearing on the problem of recognizing human faces. However, several relevant observations can be extracted. In the first two experiments, reducing the information content of pictures in certain ways (eg. compressing the grey scale) aided recognition of the pictures, and such information-reduced pictures were preferred by the subjects. This may have bearing on the design of displays for iconic communication.

Finally the third experiment describes one specialized way in which iconic data (human faces) can be encoded using a descriptor set. Although there is no reason to believe that humans would encode the data in the same way, the remarkable performance obtained from a rather small quantity of information (22 integral values from 1 to 5) is worth noting for computer-encoding of such data.

HARMON 1971B.
Leon D. Harmon -- see GOLDSTEIN 1971.

HARMON 1972.
L.D. Harmon -- see GOLDSTEIN 1972.

HAYGOOD 1965.
D. H. Haygood.
Audio-visual concept formation.
Journal of Educational Psychology 56(1965) 126-132.

In an investigation of instructional treatment by learner-variable interaction, 437 college Ss were divided between filmed and live physics lecture demonstrations. Immediate- and delayed-recall criteria were applied. Using prior knowledge of physics and 14 other learner characteristics as independent moderator variables, a series of 2 X 3 X 3 unweighted means analyses indicated that attitude toward instructional films, ascendance, responsibility, numerical aptitude, verbal aptitude, past experience with entertainment films, and past use of college library instructional films interacted significantly with instructional treatments, primarily on the immediate-recall criterion. Prior knowledge of physics modified most of these effects. Attitudes toward entertainment films and toward physics, emotional stability, sociability, total personality self-evaluation, academic achievement, and unspecified past experience with instructional films did not interact with instructional treatments. There are 15 references.

/1970/DWYER/DRE/education/visual/color/effectiveness/.

READER'S COMMENTS -- This study needs to be compared with subsequent work of Rohwer, Bugelski, and others showing that visual elaboration aids PA learning. Information here was redundant. The analysis may be affected by unequal variances.

HEBB 1968.
D. O. Hebb.
Concerning imagery.
Psychological Review 75(1968)466-77.

An attempt is made to analyze imagery in psychological terms. It is proposed (A) that eye movement has an organizing function, (B) that 1st-order cell assemblies are basis of vivid specific imagery, and (C) that higher-order assemblies are the basis of less specific imagery and non representational conceptual processes. Eidetic images, hallucinations, and hypnagogic imagery are compared with the memory image, and certain peculiarities of the memory image are discussed. There are 24 references. Abstract by author.

/1968/HEBB/KMK/psychology/imagery/.

HEIDER 1971A.
Eleanor Rosch Heider.
Natural categories.
APA Proceedings 79'th Annual Convention (1971) 43-44.

In this paper Heider presents conclusive experimental evidence that concept formation in the human mind does not occur in an arbitrary way but at least in some cases follows a naturally determined formula.

To test this idea, a special human subject was needed who had no functional concepts in some easily tested perceptual domain. The stone-age culture of Dani of New Guinea were found to lack such concepts in the areas of color and geometric form since their vocabulary was restricted to expressions for "light" and "dark" only. These people were therefore good subjects for a conclusive study on the mechanism of perceptual thinking.

In the experiments with forms, three forms, the circle, square, and equilateral triangle were chosen as the basic shapes or "natural prototypes' from which all other test forms were directly or indirectly derived. Sets of three groups of seven figures each were shown to each subject. His task was to associate a Dani word with each figure of a given group and to identify the most typical example of that group. In the first set, the most typical example of each group of figures was one of the basic shapes. Slight modifications upon these natural prototype forms produce the other shapes. In all remaining sets, however, a modified shape is the true protoype of the group, but the natural prototype is always present as a peripheral member.

The color experiment followed a similar procedure with

sets comprised of the eight basic chromatic colors. The accepted standard hue of each color served as the natural prototype around which groups were built. Four of the six sets used in the experiment contained the natural prototype colors as central or peripheral members of the group. The experimental results suggested two strong tendencies in conceptualization. Natural prototype forms and colors were learned more quickly as individuals within a group, just as groups in which these forms and colors were central were learned more quickly than the others. Of equal importance it was found that categories within a set tended to be defined in terms of variations as a natural prototype even if it was not the central but a peripheral member of that category.

The implications of these findings are extensive. If as was determined in these experiments, natural prototypes exist in the domain of colors and forms, perhaps they exist in other areas as well. Consistent with the idea, perhaps artificial prototypes once learned could bias our thinking in their direction in subsequeent concept formation. Thus, in individuals, certain artificial prototypes may behave as natural prototypes. There are 5 references. Abstract by author.

/1971/HEIDER/GGD/seen/perception/color/form/.

READER'S COMMENTS -- The presence of natural categories in visual thinking and concept formation has clear importance to iconic communications.

HEIDER 1971B.
Eleanor Rosch Heider.
On the internal structure of perceptual and semantic categories.
Paper presented at Conference on Developmental Psycholinguistics, Buffalo, NY, August, 1971.

This paper argues that psychological categories have internal structure (that is, instances of categories differ in the degree to which they are like the "focal examples" of the categories); that the nature of the structure of the perceptual categories of color and form is determined by perceptually salient "natural prototypes" and that nonperceptual semantic categories also have internal structure which affects the way they are processed. There are 38 references. Abstract by author.

/1971/HEIDER/RJJ/psychology/perception/natural/prototypes/category/.

READER'S COMMENTS -- The research is highly preliminary in nature but points clearly toward a new concept of the internal structure of categories in the brain. Heider suggests that such categories consist of central (best) examples and then peripheral (poorer) ones. She shows in several differently structured experiments that the former are learned more quickly and easily than the latter, and that, for perceptual categories, the central examples are rather constant between people both within and across cultures, suggesting natural prototypes for these perceptual categories. It may indeed be that such universal prototypes are the "words" of iconic communications, but the paper stops short of such an assertion. Finally, Heider presents an interesting new theory (only partially supported) for the mechanism whereby the brain scans a category. She suggests that central members of the category are considered first and that the response time is therefore directly related to the distance of the desired item from the central example of the category.

HENGEN 1970.
Nona Hengen.
The perception of danger in action illustrations.
AV Communication Review 18(1970)250-262.

Little is known about how people respond to visuals. This research concerns how the mind translates a still picture. One particular picture was selected where the main theme was danger. On the basis of a pilot study a cue hierarchy was posited. Primary cues were expressions of man and horse, secondary and tertiary cues were loss of control over action and in downward movement of horse and rider. Eight versions of the picture were then constructed using factorial (2X3) combinations of cues. A second set of stimulus materials was also prepared with the same figure but on skis rather than on horseback. Eighty undergraduates were asked to judge the danger of the situations in the pictures by ranking them. Significant interpretation differences resulted when cues combined to evoke impression of danger vs. cues combined to evoke impression of calm. S's in the experiment were influenced first by control, second by facial appearances (the reverse of what was suggested by the pilot study).

/1970/HENGEN/DRE/cues for interpreting pictures/.

HERBERT 1968.
Evan Herbert -- see LICKLIDER 1968.

HERSKOVITS 1963, 1966.
Melville J. Herskovits -- see SEGALL 1963, 1966.

HOFFMANN 1973.
Thomas Hoffmann.
MOGUL.
Electrical Engineering Department, Johns Hopkins University, Report No. 73-6, March 1973.

HOLT 1964.
Robert R. Holt.
Imagery: The return of the ostracized.
American Psychologist 19(1964)254-264.

In the 1890's, imagery was a major topic of scientific psychology but when studies of imageless thought revealed that problem solving and associative thinking did not go on in the full light of consciousness, a psychology not founded on the study of consciousness by introspection was clearly demanded. With the development of behaviorism in the early part of this century, imagery was ostracized as a topic of scientific concern. This introduced objective, operational methods into psychology but at the expense of excluding for several decades subjective phenomena from serious study.

In this article, the author describes how several factors have lead to the reemergence of imagery as a legitimate and challenging topic of study. Hallucinations and related phenomena have had to be considered as real events affecting the performance of astronauts piloting their vehicles for long periods of time through drastically modified and impoverished environments, deprived of the sensory pull of gravity on muscles, joints and otoliths. Human life as well as national prestige may hinge on our knowledge of the conditions that induce hallucination.

Secondly, the study of hallucinogenic drugs, their biochemistry, and the growth of psychopharmocology and deprivation research has produced a growing popular interest in such phenomena. Concurrent studies in brain research (electoencephalography, direct stimulation of the brain) have revealed objective correlates of imagery experience that have now entered into neuropsychological modeling and provided a conceptual framework in which it is no longer necessary to assume that thought processes are identical with what can be reported by the thinker.

Finally, studies of creativity and experiments on the effects of marginal and subliminal stimuli have helped to bring imagery back toward the psychological spotlight.

/*PYLYSHYN 1973/.

/1964/HOLT/WHH/psychology/imagery/history/.

READER'S COMMENTS -- Further evidence of the conflict between the public use of language and symbols and the private use of imagery in thought. Since studies of imagery seem to require that subjects translate their experience into language in order to communicate with others, such studies are in effect limited to the common intersection of imagery and language and hence, must leave the private, unverbalized (and unconscious) uses of imagery unexplored.

HOLTON 1965.

Gerald Holton.
Conveying science by visual presentation.
Education of Vision, ed. Gyorgy Kepes, George Brazilier, New York, 1965.

Three faults of scientific demonstrations are discussed: distortion, dissociation, displacement. Films depict events and are removed from physical reality experienced and understood in its full context. The author feels that models (p 57) are qualitatively far below direct viewing or movies of a natural phenomenon. Seven orders of reality are listed. There are 34 references.

/1965/HOLTON/DRE/science/education/visual/communication/.

READER'S COMMENTS -- The author deals in a naive way with philosophical and psychological matters and for no clear reason believes that the "best" mode of presentation is direct observation in a natural context. Although films are mentioned frequently, little of the discussion is relevant to iconic communication.

HOLTON 1971.
Gerald Holton.
On trying to understand scientific genius.
The American Scholar 41(1971-2)95-110.

In this fascinating essay, psychological factors discernable in Einstein's life and work are examined. Although the focus is on Einstein, it is suggested that these same remarkable factors may characterize genius generally: 1) a direct special perception of the phenomena of science as if the mind intimately matched the problem without the vehicle of intervening language; 2) a clarity and simplicity of thought that formulates the problem in just the idealized milieu needed to reveal structure previously unseen; 3) extraordinary energy and dedication to pursuing the problem to the near exclusion of satisfactions other men find irresistible; and lastly, 4) a sense of self-confidence and self-reliance that mark a genius as one of the "chosen" ones.

Pursuing these features through a psychobiographical analysis of Einstein's childhood and early development, the author documents that Einstein possessed an extraordinary kind of visual imagery that provided the main instrument for his thought processes. These image-carriers of concepts seemingly were regarded as if they had absolute reality and their truth was self-evident. For Einstein "the objects with which geometry deals seemed to be of no different type than the objects of sensory perception which can be seen and touched." Holton describes the great influence of the Kanton Schule at Aarau which Einstein entered in his 15th year. This school employed Pestalozzi's approach to education--that "conceptual thinking is built on visual understanding" and that the ABC of visual understanding should be put ahead of the ABC of letters. There are 24 references and notes.

/1971/HOLTON/WHH/education/iconic/intelligence/.

READER'S COMMENTS -- What is seen enjoys the property of being perceived as "really there," whereas ideas and impressions communicated via language and symbols must ultimately be recognized as constructions of the mind that lack the phenomenally absolute character of the visual image. Could it be that by "thinking" in terms of images and other direct sensory experiences (rather than language) genius is able to build with absolute confidence creations beyond that sustainable by ordinary mortals using words and symbols which lack such absolute reality?

HUDSON 1960.
W. Hudson.
Pictorial depth perception in sub-cultural groups in Africa.
Journal of Social Psychology 52(1960)183-208.

Pictures constructed to provide self-evident responses of 2D or 3D perception on the depth cues of object size, superimposition and perspective were given to 11 samples, six of them school-going (3 white, 3 black) and five of them non-school-going (1 white, 4 black). School-going samples saw predominantly three-dimensionally, the others almost entirely two-dimensionally both in outline drawings and on a photogragh. The hypothesis that their dimensional perception was an artifact of test construction was rejected. Formal schooling and informal training combined to supply an exposure threshold necessary for the development of the process. Cultural isolation was effective in preventing or retarding the process, even in candidates possessing formal education of an advanced level. An intelligence threshold existed also for the process, but its development with candidates of average or higher intellectual endowment depended upon exposure to the specific experience and probably upon cultural characteristics which in Africa might have genetic perceptual determinants. The implications of the findings on advertisements and propaganda and on all didactic pictorial material were discussed. There are 17 references. Abstract by author.

/1960/HUDSON/DRE/anthropology/primitive/spatial/perception/.

READER'S COMMENTS -- It is not clear to what extent the results may be biased by testing conditions.

HUGGINS 1966.
W.H. Huggins and Donald Weiner.
HARMONIC PHASORS--I.
Education Development Center, Inc., 55 Chapel Street, Newton, Mass.

HARMONIC PHASORS is a computer pantomime designed for use as a teaching aid to demonstrate without using words and equations how:

1. sinusoidal motion may be represented by projecting uniform circular motion upon a line;
2. special properties result when the frequencies of the motions are harmonically related in proportion to the integers 0, 1, 2, etc.;
3. the projection of the sum of several circular motions is equal to the sum of their individual projections;
4. the sum of the harmonic motions yields a resultant which has the same period as the fundamental component but is more complicated in waveform;
5. a periodic train of impulses may be approximated by the sum of several harmonic components that all reach their maximum values at the same instant.

These ideas are relevant to the description of a periodic function by Fourier series; the representation of sinusoidal signals by rotating "phasors"; and the addition of vector quantities, generally.

It is intended that the film be shown twice, with no prior commentary or concurrent discussion during the first showing, following which all viewers should be asked to describe what they had just seen. From this discussion, the principles demonstrated by the film may be summarized and then the film viewed again.

By omitting a sound track and printed titles on the film, the instructor using the film has the opportunity to discuss these ideas in the context of particular subject matter to which they relate, using his own terminology, and mode of expression.

READER'S COMMENTS -- This 7 minute, black and white, silent film was produced for the National Committee for Electrical Engineering Films under a grant from the National Science Foundation. (Released 1966) The film is available for rent or purchase from the Educational Development Center.

HUGGINS 1967.
W.H. Huggins
Film animation by computer.
Mechanical Engineering 89(1967)26-29.

Computers are machines that read, create, and manipulate symbols. By using the computer to generate pictures -- to make movies -- one can clarify and demonstrate concepts that are difficult to show with traditional apparatus. There are 6 references. Abstract by author.

/1967/HUGGINS/computer/animation/demonstration/.

HUGGINS 1968A.
William H. Huggins and Doris R. Entwisle.
Exploratory studies of films for engineering education.
Final report, Grant NO. OEG2-7-062816-3097, Office of Education, U.S. Department of Health, Education and Welfare, under Project NO. 6-2816. 1968, The Johns Hopkins University,Baltimore, Md 21218.

The original purpose of this research was to explore, by way of a pilot study, the effectiveness of two films especially developed to teach the same topic. Both films are directed toward explicating the relationship between voltages and currents in an electrical circuit. One film, an animated version, is like a cartoon. A second film covering the same material is a conventional studio film that photographs a demonstration involving actual physical equipment. A film of this demonstration was undertaken initially because it involved rather complicated and expensive equipment -- few colleges would find it reasonable to produce it "live'. The National Committee on Electrical Engineering Films sponsored this film as the first of a series concerned with the general concept of linearity. The difficulties that emerged, however, encouraged the authors to attempt another film made by computer-animation. The research reported is an outgrowth of that endeavor.

After the animated film was produced it seemed so obviously superior to the conventional film that to conduct a full-blown field test of a relative worth of the two films would have been wasteful. Several other films (see below) were therefore produced to explore new dimensions of the problem. Detailed field and experimental tests were made with one short film (Dynamic Symbols) developed expressly for test purposes. Also considerable attention was given to programming languages and to notational conventions in relation to computer produced films. The original purpose of this research was thus modified and considerably expanded.

Some of the findings discussed in this report are the following:

1) Electric circuits provide subject matter of unusual interest for studying the perception of abstract relations. They obey simple logical rules. They have both quantitative and topological properties. Furthermore, the existence of dual relations permits different but logically equivalent presentations to be made of many of the important ideas.

2) A new symbolic convention for showing the current through an element and tne voltage across it is demonstrated and compared with the traditional meter. In particular, this new meter symbol allows one to show simutaneously the values of many signals in the system, as is demonstrated by the computer-animated film by Eugene Stull. Other symbols of an abstract nature are introduced to represent active and passive elements and their properties are demonstrated in a set of pilot films. These innovations may be useful for CAI displays.

3) Whereas undergraduate day-students subjects in the first field test found the abstract film amusing and laughed frequently, in an identical test older evening students showed absolutely no amusement. Besides raising the question whether a classroom presentation that appeals to the young full-time student will appeal to the older part-time student, this replicates conclusions of other researchers that interactive rather than simple effects should be studied.

4) A comparison of the effectiveness of a movie with a sequence of still slides made from selected frames in the movie showed that the additional information provided by the movie over the sequence of still slides was assimilated better by the students majoring in engineering and science than by those in liberal arts.

5) Some evidence suggested that pictorial associations to an object may be unrelated to the verbal associations. This is an important topic that needs further investigation.

6) The relation of this work to current studies in cognition and linguistics points up the importance of developing more effective means for visualizing relations, especially by stripping off realistic, but irrelevant, detail.

Accompanying this final report to the Office of Education were four reels of film:

1) "A Geometric View of a Resistor Circuit" by Grayson (10.5 minute 16-mm black and white film). This reel contains an edited version of the original Grayson film made in the studios of the Educational Development Center (formerly ESI), Newton, Massachusetts, followed immediately by a computer-animated version by Beck that attempts to reproduce the same scenes as closely as possible.

2) "A Geometric View of a Resistor Circuit" by Stull (6 minute 16-mm black and white film). This is the intial effort to display the same concepts as the original Grayson film, but using the new meter symbol. In this film the linear additive feature of the current meter is used to demonstrate Kirchhoff's current law, and other conventions are explored.

3) "Pythagorean Film" an exercise in computer-animation to demonstrate the Pythagorean Theorem for a 3:4:5 triangle (2 minutes) by Dennis Knepp.

4) "Pilot Films for Abstract Symbols' (12 minutes, 16-mm black and white film). A collection of eight computer-animated films showing concepts relating to voltage and current in series and parallel circuits with abstract and realistic symbols.

The single, polished film to emerge from this program, which was used in the field test, and which may be of interest to others who are working on research in visual cognition, is "Dynamic Symbols" (3-1/2 minute 16-mm black and white film). It is on deposit at the Education Developmentepartment Center, Newton, Massachusetts and a print may be obtained by contacting that Center.

HUGGINS 1968B.
W.H. Huggins and Doris R. Entwisle.
Introductory Systems and Design.
Ginn/Blaisdell, Waltham, Mass., 1968.

A largely self-teaching introductory text on systems in which a major effort has been made to relate conventional algebraic descriptions to flow-graph representations which are believed by the authors to have helpful iconic properties useful for portraying abstract system structure and signal relationships.

/1968/HUGGINS/ENTWISLE/WHH/systems/education/engineering/representation/model/.

HUGGINS 1971.
William H. Huggins.
Iconic Communications.
IEEE Transactions on Education 14(1971) 158-163.

The computer has been viewed primarily as a symbol-manipulating machine. Yet, it is capable of generating and displaying visual images showing abstract form, shape, and dynamic process. Recent psychological research on perception suggests that pictures and symbols play important but very different roles in creative thought. By providing enactive and iconic modes of communication between man and machine, the computer can serve as a prosthetic device to assist man in giving public expression to his private mental images. By so doing, it may be possible to equalize in some measure the great imbalance between man's great endowment for perceiving and very limited capacity for producing visual images. By so doing, we may enhance the human use of the computer as an intellectual companion rather than as an economic competitor. Abstract by author.

/1971/HUGGINS/symbols/computer/images/.

HUGGINS 1973A.
W.H. Huggins -- see ENTWISLE 1973A.

HUGGINS 1973B.
W.H. Huggins.
HARMONIC PHASORS--II.
Education Development Center, 55 Chapel Street, Newton, Mass.

This computer-animated film is a sequel to HARMONIC PHASORS--I using the same visual conventions as used in the earlier film to explain how complex periodic waveforms may be described by superposition of simpler cirular motions having harmonically related frequencies.

By combining spoken narrative with carefully designed iconic explications, several aspects of Fourier theory are shown visually:

1. Waveshape depends critically on choice of harmonic components, their amplitudes and phases.

2. A phase shift proportional to the frequency of each component creates a simple time-delay in the resulting waveform.

3. Gibbs' effect is a kind of phasor whiplash that occurs when approximating any discontinuity.

4. The Hilbert transform of a waveform is found by increasing the initial angle of all phasors by 90 degrees.

5. Fejer summation gives less weight to higher harmonics and eliminates the Gibbs' effect.

6. Gibbs' effect is also eliminated by "cosine" and "cosine-squared" weighting schemes.

7. These ideas are illustrated using a wide variety of waveforms including: a waveform which is its own Hilbert transform; a periodic train of impulses; a sinewave and a cosinewave; a squarewave; a sawtooth wave; a monopolar pulse; a bipolar pulse; a rectified sinewave.

All images in the film (including the titles) were created in a single run of 90-min. duration on an IBM-7094 computer. This 17-minute, white-on-blue, 16-mm sound film was produced by Education Development Center, Newton, Mass. for the National Committee for Electrical Engineering Films with the support of the National Science Foundation. The FORTRAN-compatible movie language M*O*G*U*L was developed (HOFFMANN 1973) at Johns Hopkins under NSF grant GJ-336.

HUTTENLOCHER 1968.
Janellen Huttenlocher.
Constructing spatial images: a strategy in reasoning.
Psychological Review 75(1968)550-560.

This paper describes how persons construct images to solve 3-term series problems. (If A is bigger than B, and C is smaller than B, which is taller?) Depending upon how such problems are phrased, their difficulty varies. People claim that they construct imaginary spatial arrays to solve these problems but are ashamed of this strategy. Subjects easily assign spatial axes to nonspatial dimensions and then arrange the "object" along these dimensions. This strategy explains observed variations in the difficulty of alternative forms of these problems. There are 5 references.

/1968/HUTTENLOCHER/DRE/spatial/cognition/image/structure/.

HWANG 1971.
R.C. Hwang -- see TALBOT 1971.

IRWIN 1968.
Ruth Beckey Irwin and Aleki Nickles.
The efficacy of sound motion pictures as instructional media.
Unpublished Ohio State University Research Report, Feb. 1968.

The assumption was made that instructional films in speech pathology were needed to meet the needs of students in preparation for clinical practice. Principal objectives were (1) To produce short films on treatment of misarticulations, (2) To evaluate effectiveness of these films as supplements to classroom instruction and (3) To prepare tests and study materials to accompany the films.

Procedures were concerned with production, evaluation, and preparation of materials. Clinicians and subjects were selected to meet requirements of scripts. Tests based on films were prepared. Three experimental groups were selected to test validity of tests and films. Members of one group were retested after limited training. A fourth group was evaluated following classroom lectures supplemented by the films.

Four short films (16 mm sound movies in black and white) on misarticulations were the principal products. In addition, film cartridges (8 mm) are available for use in Technicolor Super 8 Sound Projector.

Principal significant findings were as follows: (1) Film tests of observational accuracy differentiated between experienced and inexperienced groups; (2) Experienced clinicians were more accurate observers of therapy than other groups (Films 1 and 2); (3) Classroom lectures supplemented by viewing Film 1 were effective in improvement of visual, acoustic, and therapeutic observational accuracy; (4) Visual and acoustic observational accuracy were related to total scores (visual, acoustic, therapeutic).

It would appear that instructional films have significant implications for instruction of clinical methods in speech pathology as supplement to lectures and "live demonstrations". There are 14 references. Abstract by authors.

/1968/IRWIN/NICKLES/PKF/communication/speech/film/.

JAHODA 1970.
G. Jahoda and B. Stacey.
Susceptibility to geometrical illusions according to culture and professional training.

Perception and Psychophysics 7(1970) 179-184.

This paper reports a cross-cultural investigation of susceptibility to geometrical illusions based upon student samples in Ghana and Scotland. The results indicate that: (1) Cultural differences in susceptibility to illusions can be found among Ss exposed to lengthy formal education of a similar type; (2) The perceptual consequences of professional training in art and architecture tend to be moderate within a culture; but (3) The combined outcome of training across cultures tends to reduce cultural differences in susceptibility to illusions. They also raise a problem concerning the supposed positive relationship between field dependence and susceptibility to illusions. Some implications of these results are considered. There are 26 references. Abstract by author.

/1970/JAHODA/STACEY/DRE/culture/illusions/.

JENKINS 1967.
J.R. Jenkins, D.C. Neale, and S.L. Deno.
Differential memory to a picture and word stimuli.
Journal of Educational Psychology 58(1967) 303-307.

The data confirm that pictures are more easily remembered than words. The free-association data suggest that associations to a word are different from associations to its pictorial representation. Associative overlap was of lesser magnitude between sets of words than between sets of pictures. To compare the effects of using either pictures or words in a recognition task, 120 college sophomores were assigned randomly to 4 treatment conditions: (A) See pictures -- recognize pictures (PP); (B) See words -- recognize words (WW); (C) See pictures -- recognize words (PW); (D) See words -- recognize pictures (WP). When the number of correct identifications of the original stimuli were compared, Group PP was superior to WW, And PW was virtually the same as WW but significantly superior to WP. The tendency to admit intrusions, identifying new stimuli as members of the initial series, was significantly more predominant in the WW condition than in the PP condition. Results were discussed in relation to hypotheses about the nature of encoding processes for pictures and words. There are 8 references. Abstract by author.

/1967/JENKINS/NEALE/DENO/DRE/education/psychology/picture/word/memory/.

JENKINS 1969.
J.R. Jenkins, W.B. Stack, and S.L. Deno.
Children's recognition and recall of picture and word stimuli.
AV Communication Review 17(1969) 265-271.

Using black-white line drawings, the authors tested second-grade children's recall and recognition of picture stimuli and word stimuli. Recall measures show no difference by mode of presentation, although recall scores are related to reading level (IQ?) scores. Recognition of pictures was superior to recognition of words (about 2 items out of 17), and fewer intrusions were found with pictures. There are 10 references.

/1969/JENKINS/STACK/DENO/DRE/education/psychology/memory/picture/word/.

READER'S COMMENTS -- This is a minimal test since the pictures are not very multidimensional.

JONIDES 1971, 1972.
John Jonides -- see EGETH 1971, 1972.

JULESZ 1966.
Bela Julesz.
Binocular disappearance of monocular symmetry.
Science 153(1966) 657-658.

In an earlier demonstration binocular shapes were produced from monocularly shapeless, random-dot stereo images. A reversal of this phenomenon is demonstrated. A stereo image is devised in which the monocularly apparent shapes of bilateral symmetry disappear when stereoscopically viewed. This phenomenon sharpens the implications of the earlier one. There are 2 references. Abstract by author.

/1966/JULESZ/psychology/vision/stereo/.

JULESZ 1971.
Bela Julesz.
Foundations of Cyclopean Perception.
The University of Chicago Press, Chicago, 1971.

The anaglyphs presented here belong to a unique class of computer-generated visual stimuli, the random-dot correlogram, which was first produced by Bela Julesz in 1959 and has since become a paradigm for research in vision and perception. Containing no monocular patterns, the correlogram cues the cyclopean retina alone, and skips operationally the anatomical retinae.

"Here there is a sharp, determinate, distinctive perception of form that must originate somewhere in the visual nervous system beyond the retinae of the eyes. As psychologists, then, we have to a certain extent managed to look into the "black box" of the visual system: we have found out something about where a particular perceptual process takes place. This is a procedure that is seldom employed in the traditional experimental psychology of perception," Julesz writes.

This study defines cyclopean methodology as the "formation of a percept at some central location in the visual system by using stimuli that could not possibly produce that percept at an earlier location," and generalizes both the technique of random-dot stereograms and the conception of the cyclopean retina. Published after a decade of research by the author and other workers in the field of visual perception, Foundations of Cyclopean Perception relates, as no other work has done, current research in such areas as experimental psychology, neurophysiology, mathematical models, and computer graphics. The superbly reproduced correlograms, including over one hundred black-and-white stereograms and one hundred colored anaglyphs, demonstrate the author's findings.

This work traces the information flow in the visual system, with particular emphasis upon the separation of peripheral, or retinal, processes from central, or cerebral, ones. This program of process localization is carried out for some of the main experiments in visual perception such as optical illusions, simultaneous contrast phenomena and aftereffects of movement and depth. The main findings of cyclopean perception in the context of neuroanatomical and nurophysiological evidnece are reviewed and in addition, the book summarizes the advances in monocular and binocular perception obtained by the use of random textures that have resulted in the model of stereopses developed by Julesz and others and published here for the first time.

The study has rich implications both for immediate use and for further research. Cyclopean methodology has already helped to solve problems ranging from brain lesions to eidetic memory. The anaglyphs presented here will serve as clinical test plates for locating and quantifying stereopsis deficiency, and the book includes a discussion of other clinical uses of cyclopean techniques.

"This important original, and distinctive book is a most significant contribution to the body of knowledge and theory in human perception." Abstract by Benjamin White, San Francisco State College. 414 references.

/1971/JULESZ/JW/psychology/perception/computer graphics/.

READER'S COMMENTS -- Excellent treatise on visual perception wherein the stimuli are computer generated random dot stereograms.

KADANOFF 1969.
Leo P. Kadanoff, Jerrold R. Voss and Wendell J. Bouknight.
A city grows before your eyes.
Computer Decisions (Dec 1969) 16-23.

Dynamic modelling of urban growth is achieved by coupling a graphic display to a computer which stores real estate and land use data. There are 17 references. Abstract by author.

/1969/KADANOFF/VOSS/BOUKNIGHT/RJJ/graphics/simulation/maps/applications/.

READER'S COMMENTS -- A good example of a practical use of iconics, specifically a moving graphic display, as the output mechanism for an urban simulation. In fact, the simulation system is not completed, but the output system is here demonstrated anyway.

KAGAN 1970A.
Jerome Kagan.
Attention and psychological change in the young child.

Science 170(1970)826-832.

One developmental phenomenon involves the initial establishment and subsequent alteration of representations of experience (schemata). Experimental observations of infants suggest that the human face is one of the earliest representations to be acquired. There is behavioral addiction to contour and movement. There is a preferential orientation to change that is clearly adaptive, for the locus of change is likely to contain the most information about the presence of a mother or of danger. Sometime during the second month, duration of attention comes under the influence of the relation between a class of events and the infant's schema for that class. ("High rate of change" is displaced by "discrepancy"). Toward the end of the first year a new cognitive structure (the hypothesis) emerges -- the child interprets a discrepant event by mentally transforming it to a form he is already familiar with -- the structure is the hypothesis. Quantification of the fragile process of attention is still inelegant. There are 35 references.

/1970/KAGAN/DRE/psychology/attention/.

KAGAN 1970B.
Jerome Kagan.
The determinants of attention in the infant.
American Scientist 58(1970)298-306.

Much attention is now directed to the mental processes of the young child. Since acquiring knowledge about the environment depends so intimately upon how the infant distributes his attention, and for how long, it is important to ask what governs this.

Stimuli that move or possess light-dark contrast are most likely to attract and hold a new-born's attention. There is an initial disposition to attend to events, visual or auditory, with a high rate of change. The notion of schema helps explain the older infant's distribution of attention. Events moderately discrepant from his schema elicit longer fixations than very familiar or very novel events. (The discrepancy hypothesis.) A curvilinear relation between attention and stimulus-schema discrepancy is supported by both observational and experimental data.

Toward the end of the first year hypotheses develop. These are interpretations of some experience accomplished by mentally transforming an unusual event to the form the child is familiar with. Activation of hypotheses determine length of attention in older infants.

Sex and social class differences in fixation time are discussed. The central problem in educating children, it is stated, is to attract and maintain focused attention.

Evidence is cited in this paper of the remarkable memory for pictures noted by Haber. An average 4-year-old can correctly recall 45 out of 50 pictures. There are 29 references.

/1970/KAGAN/DRE/psychology/attention/education/picture/memory/.

READER'S COMMENTS -- This article suggests why iconic communication may be an efficient mode of communication.

KAHNE 1969.
Merton J. Kahne, Judah L. Schwartz, and Michael Knudsen.
Slides: a dictionary system for computer study of graphic or pictorial displays.
Behavioral Science 14(1969) 418-427.

This paper describes a general purpose filing system which permits a user to assign labels to particular objects or a group of objects in any of a large number of photographic slides. Stored in a computer in the form of a "dictionary", the information can be used to drive a carousel type projector in synchrony with an unfolding "dialogue" which takes place at a teletype console between a computer user and his machine. The system makes it possible to incorporate photographically organized pictorial, graphic, or diagrammatic information into computer programs without having to resort to complex programming. An example of one type of implementation is given to illustrate special features and potentialities of the system. This is accompanied by a discussion of the rationale employed as well as a detailed description of key functions used in manipulating the slides data in conjunction with other computer generated information. The flexibility achieved through the creation of the dictionary makes the system particularly attractive as a research tool, since it not only permits the researcher to use pictorial material in intimate interaction with sophisticated natural language interchanges, but it also provides a simple vehicle to test alternative strategies or materials without extensive programming. Finally, it may be used as an aid in attempts to evaluate pictorial material using the computer's computational and logical decision-making capacity. There are 5 references. Abstract by author.

/1969/KAHNE/SCHWARTZ/KNUDSEN/DRE/computer/graphic/device/system/.

READER'S COMMENTS -- Clever, relatively inexpensive system which would appear particularly useful in teaching. In addition to its basic cost saving feature, the system allows half-tone and color pictures to be displayed.

KALLIS 1969.
Stephen A. Kallis, Jr.
Motion picture animation by computer.
Computers and Automation (Nov 1969) 30-34.

The computer is used to control the movements of the animation stand as well as the animation camera in the scheme described in this paper. A general review of methods to perform film animation is presented: Zajac's computer graphics with a slave camera (below professional quality, but quick and cheap enough for an instructional medium) versus the cartoon studio with hand animation (good quality but very expensive). The computer can aid in the latter process by either on-line or off-line controlling the animation stand and camera, saving the animator substantial amounts of time. The obvious drawbacks of the systems described are the large investments in programming and digital control mechanisms required.

/1969/KALLIS/SMZ/computer/animation/system/.

KAMIYA 1953.
J. Kamiya -- see BRUNSWIK 1953.

KATZMAN 1972.
Natan Katzman and James Nygenhuis.
Color vs black and white effects on learning, opinion and attention.
AV Communication Review 20(1972) 16-23.

The addition of color to an audiovisual presentation caused subjects in two experiments to recall significantly more of the peripheral material presented by non-verbal cues. Central material (media content relevant to the basic information, message, plot, or theme) and verbal material presented in captions or voice balloons, were not affected by color. There is weak evidence that color presentations are seen as more active, interesting, and emotional. There are 5 references.

/1972/KATZMAN/DRE/graphics/display/color/differences/.

READER'S COMMENTS -- This paper is in line with the general hypothesis that color adds little to the effectiveness of films.

KEPES 1966.
Gyorgy Kepes, editor.
Sign, Image, Symbol.
George Braziller, New York, 1966.

Sixth in a series of volumes dedicated to the search for values common to our contemporary scientific, technological and artistic achievements.

These books are organized around the premise that vision is a fundamental aspect of human insight and that all creative thinking is based upon the ability to see in a clearer, broader, more coherent way than before.

Communication, in its broadest sense, is the subject of the present volume. Different aspects of comprehension, observation, perception, and representation are here studied by scientists, psychologists, historians, anthropologists, architects, and artists. The essays establish a broad interpretation of the meaning of signs, images, and symbols, and explore the creative uses of image-making and symbol-making in the encoding of our common culture and the shaping of our environment.

/1966/KEPES/WHH/anthropology/art/graphics/language/communication/design/vision/imagery/symbol/.

READER'S COMMENTS -- The 21 essays comprising this volume are lavishly illustrated. A delightful book to read!

KILBRIDE 1968A.
P.L. Kilbride and M.C. Robbins.
Linear perspective, pictorial depth perception and education among the Baganda.
Perceptual and Motor Skills 27(1968) 601-602.

Depth perception, which seems to be related to education, is based on several cues, one being linear perspective. This report studies the association between education and linear perspective in Baganda (Uganda) children (N=242) and adults (N=281) whose education ranged from none to about 8 years. For each group separately, there is significant association between amount of education and perceiving linear perspective in 2 cards drawn from Hudson's depth perception test. There are 4 references.

/1968/KILBRIDE/ROBBINS/DRE/spatial/perception/anthropology/perspective/.

READER'S COMMENTS -- Although subjects were tested with 4 test cards, results for only 2 cards are reported.

KILBRIDE 1968B.
P.L. Kilbride, M.C. Robbins and R.B. Freeman.
Pictorial depth perception and education among Baganda school children.
Perceptual and Motor Skills 26(1968) 1116-1118.

The relative amount of pictorial perception of depth among rural Baganda school children was directly related to amount of formal education. Use of superposition as a cue to pictorial depth perception appeared to be less dependent on education than object size and perhaps other cues. There are 3 references. Abstract by author.

/1968/KILBRIDE/DRE/anthropology/spatial/perception/schooling/primitive/.

READER'S COMMENTS -- These conclusions are open to question since there is no unschooled comparison group. It appears that age varied from 4 to 20 years, and schooling varied from early primary to late secondary. Age as well as schooling could account for the findings. The authors' statement- "These relationships obtained despite a stratified sampling control of age" is unclear and is not borne out in the data presentation.

KNOWLTON,JQ 1966.
James Q. Knowlton.
On the definition of "picture".
AV Communication Review 14(1966) 157-183.

This is a discussion (no data) of "syntax of film" or "film grammar," starting from the earlier Pryluck and Snow (1967) paper defining the basic element as the kind of information -- digital or analogic -- transmitted. An analytical model of filmic communication is proposed. Digital or analogic information in the environment is coded (shot), then recorded (edited picture), until finally a general symbol system emerges (film, edited sequence); the film is then displayed. The difference in logical structure between language and film is reflected in the sequencing of primary coding units (words vs shots). There is a general absence of devices to signal relationships between shots. The general problem of multiple tracks (sound, music, word, picture) is raised.

The writer describes a beginning attempt to set forth a taxonomy of visual-iconic signs of a sort that is independent of the physical attributes of the sign vehicles thus categorized. This requires that a visual-iconic sign be analyzed in a way that takes account of the verbal context in which it is embedded.

A visual-iconic representation can be thought of as having three "parts": the elements, their pattern or arrangement, and their order of connection. A visual representation will here be regarded as iconic if at least one of its three categories of "parts" -- elements, spatial arrangement of elements, or order of connection of elements -- is nonarbitrary. Any one, or all, of the three "parts' of a visual representation can represent a corresponding aspect of a state of affairs in any one of three ways: realistically, by analogy (as explained below), or artitrarily.

1. Realistic pictures. When the need is to represent some state of affairs of a sort that is visually perceivable either directly or with technological aid (eg microscope, time-lapse photography).

2. Analogical pictures. One might illustrate how the muscles are attached to (and articulate) the bones of the skeleton by using realistic pictures of muscles connected to bones. Although such an illustration portrays objects in the visual world, these objects are portrayed only in order to show the nature of a structure or process.

3. Logical pictures. When "schematization" is carried to its logically furthest extreme, the elements in the state of affairs represented are represented in a totally arbitrary fashion. When this occurs, one has what is here called a logical picture: a visual representation wherein the elements are arbitrarily portrayed, while pattern and/or order of connection are isomorphic with the state of affairs represented. There are 20 references.

/1966/KNOWLTON,JQ/DRE/communication/engineering/representation/picture/language/.

READER'S COMMENTS -- This is a discussion with no actual data.

KNOWLTON,KC 1964.
Kenneth C. Knowlton.
A computer technique for producing animated movies.

Proceedings of the American Federation Information Processing Societies Joint Spring Computer Conference 25(1964)67-87.

This paper describes a computer technique for the production of animated movies using a special programming language BEFLIX that contains such instructions as ZOOM, COPY, PAINT, DISOLV. This paper describes a 17-minute 16mm black and white silent movie which was produced by the very process which it describes. The movie has become a classic that for the first time shows the powerful capabilities of the computer to use a special problem-oriented language for producing visual images. This film (of the same title) is available on loan from Bell Telephone Laboratories, Inc., Murray Hill, New Jersey.

/*WEINER 1968/*WEINER 1971/*KNOWLTON 1965/*KNOWLTON 1968/ KNOWLTON 1969/*KNOWLTON 1970/.

/1964/KNOWLTON/WHH/computer/program/graphics/application/ animation/language/halftone/film/.

READER'S COMMENTS -- An early, important paper and film that is still a remarkable tour de force.

KNOWLTON,KC 1965.
Kenneth C. Knowlton.
Computer-produced movies.
Science 150(1965)1116-1120.

This paper gives an excellent summary of the advantages and potential capabilities of using a computer-controlled display tube and camera to produce animated movies quickly and economically. A natural application is to display the results of a computer simulation of some model. 6 references.

/*WEINER 1971/*KNOWLTON 1972/.

/1965/KNOWLTON/WHH/computer/graphics/animation/film/education/simulation/.

KNOWLTON,KC 1967.
Kenneth C. Knowlton.
Computer-animated movies.
Emerging Concepts in Computer Graphics(ed. by Don Secrest and Jurg Nievergelt,
W.A. Benjamin, New York, 1968.

Computer-produced movies are playing an increasing role in technical education and research. A dozen computer films, made at Bell Labs during the period 1963-67, are cited as demonstrating the dynamic graphical power of computers and automated film-recording equipment. Movies made by computer are seen to be a significant adjunct to education and scientific investigation, particularly in areas amenable to mathematical and logical treatment, and where results can or should be visualized. Included is a listing of films available on loan. There are 18 references. Abstract by author.

/1967/KNOWLTON,KC/SMZ/education/animation/cinema/.

READER'S COMMENTS -- The author gives a brief review of several computer animated films produced at Bell Labs. The original purpose for and outcome of each film is mentioned. A summary of the computer-animation effort and its relative advantages over other methods is given. The impression one gets from the reviews is that the early films only discovered but did not exploit the advantages of computer animation.

KNOWLTON,KC 1969A.
Kenneth C. Knowlton -- see HARMON 1969.

KNOWLTON,KC 1969B.
Kenneth C. Knowlton and Lorinda L. Cherry.
FORTRAN IV BEFLIX.
Proceedings of 9th Annual UIDE Meeting, San Diego, Calif., Nov 1969.

A description of a slightly revised BEFLIX movie language (KNOWLTON 1964) programmed in FORTRAN IV in order to make it machine independent and to permit easy combination of normal mathematical and line-drawing capabilities of FORTRAN with the area-filling and grey-scale facilities of BEFLIX.

/*KNOWLTON 1970A/.

/1969/KNOWLTON/CHERRY/WHH/computer/program/graphics/animation/language/film/halftone/.

KNOWLTON,KC 1970A.
Kenneth C. Knowlton.
EXPLOR--a generator of images from Explicit Patterns, Local Operations, and Randomness.
Proceedings of 9th Annual UAIDE meeting, Miami Beach, Florida, 1970.

EXPLOR is a system for computer-generation of still or moving images from explicitly defined patterns, local operations, and randomness. Output images are rectangular arrays (240 x 340) of black, white, and "twinkling" dots; internally, information for each position is encoded as an alphanumeric character.

Scientific and artistic applications include the production of stimuli for visual experiments, the depiction of visual "phosphenes' such as moving checkerboards and stripes, and picture processing. The system may also be used to simulate a variety of two-dimensional processes and mechanisms, such as crystal growth and etching, neural (e.g. retinal) nets, random walk, diffusion, and iterative arrays of logic modules, There are 6 references and 9 detailed figures showing various textures and patterns produced by EXPLOR.

/*KNOWLTON 1972/.

/1970/KNOWLTON/WHH/computer/graphics/language/pattern/shading/structure/art/.

KNOWLTON,KC 1971.
Kenneth C. Knowlton.
TARPS--A two-dimensional alphanumeric roster picture system. Proceedings of the 10th Annual UAIDE meeting, Los Angeles, Calif., Oct. 1971.

A description of TARPS (Two-dimensional Alphanumeric Roster Picture System) for the production of designs, diagrams, and textures, usually for movies. The paper presents the language in programmer's manual form and includes sample outputs. This is the system used by Vanderbeek to produce the short films "Poemfield No 1 through No 8."

/1971/KNOWLTON/WHH/computer/graphics/language/pattern/shading/art/.

KNOWLTON,KC 1972.
Kenneth C. Knowlton.
Collaborations with artists--a programmer's reflections. Graphics Languages, editors F. Nake and A. Rosenfeld, North-Holland Publishing Company, Amsterdam, London, 1972.

A personal review by one of the leaders in computer animation of his experiences in working with Stan Vanderbeek and Lillian Schwartz to produce new visual art forms. He concludes that "the way to true art by means of computers is not easy for two reasons. The first is that programmers and artists experience the world and their tools in quite different ways." But more fundamental is the resolution of the following dilemma: "We would like to explore the very wide variety of possible ways of describing and producing graphics. But any use of these ways can become an artistic medium only if it is developed in depth to the point where artists and viewers alike can have enough common experience to get their bearings in this particular space of possibilities.... Both artist and viewer thus need sufficient familiarity with the set of possible pictures in any one system for the message to be more than simply the medium."

The paper gives 6 references to the art films and related papers.

/1972/KNOWLTON/WHH/computer/art/application/cimema/.

READER'S COMMENTS -- Knowlton's experience provides clear cut evidence of the fundamental problem of iconic communication: That the development of new visual forms must take into account the viewer as well as the producer of the images. But, because these possibilities are so enormously varied, some theoretical guide lines are desperately needed to select the most promising possibilities.

KNOWLTON,KC 1973.
Kenneth C. Knowlton.
Computer films.
Filmmakers Newsletter 4(Dec 1970)14-20. 80 Wooster Street, New York, N.Y. 10012.

This article is based on a lecture given by Dr. Knowlton at EAT (Experiments in Art and Technology), in March 1968. It discusses the problems of working at the art-technology interface.

/*KNOWLTON 1972/.

/1970/KNOWLTON/WHH/computer/art/application/cimema/.

KNUDSEN 1969.
Michael Knudsen -- see KAHNE 1969.

KOLERS 1968.
Paul A. Kolers.
Some psychological aspects of pattern recognition.
Recognizing Patterns--Studies in Living and Automatic Systems, edited by Paul A. Kolers and Murray Eden, The M.I.T. Press, Cambridge, Mass., Chapter 1 (1966) 4-61.

A concise review of some of the perceptual phenomena psychologists have studied that are relevant to pattern recognition. The author emphasizes that human pattern perception is characterized by generative, constructive processes the perceiver supplies to inputs he selects for attention. Some of these depend on the timing and geometrical form of the inputs, but others involve cognitive factors, conceptions, ideas, wishes and plans. There are 126 references.

/1968/KOLERS/WHH/psychology/visual/pattern/recognition/.

READER'S COMMENTS -- The emphasis on the generative rules for producing patterns (pattern conception) due to Miller and Chomsky is appealing and would seem to be highly relevant to the study of iconics.

KOLERS 1969A.
Paul A. Kolers.
Reading pictures: some cognitive aspects of visual perception.
In T.S. Huang and O.J. Tretiak (eds.) Picture Band Width Comparison, New York: Gordon and Breach (1972) 97-126.

Engineers concerned with picture-processing have found it useful to familiarize themselves with some of the literature on response characteristics of the human eye. Although these more biophysical parameters must be considered in designing a suitable television-transmission system, still other parameters characterize the way people look at pictures. Some aspects of the more cognitive component of looking at pictures are described, and suggestions are made for how data of this kind could be used to save on bandwidth. There are 20 references. Abstract by author.

/*KOLERS 1969B/

/1969/KOLERS/psychology/visual/cognition/picture/.

KOLERS 1969B.
Paul A. Kolers.
The role of shape and geometry in picture recognition.
In B.S. Lipkin and A. Rosenfeld (eds.) Picture Processing and Psychopictorics, New York: Gordon and Breach (1972)97-124.

A question that has guided a great deal of research into visual perception is whether a small set of visual attributes can be defined whose combination yields percepts. I have described three approaches to this question -- mental chemistry, Gestalt psychology, and the current approach called the psychophysics of form perception. Because all three approaches have been unsuccessful in finding a set of visual "primitives' I have suggested that we turn our attention to visual operations -- the transformational characteristics of the visual system -- rather than continue to seek the "elements' on which it operates. The level of description of possible elements is likely to be far more abstract than can profitably be encompassed with a vocabulary based upon plane geometry. This fact by itself should induce investigators to examine operators. There are 31 references. Abstract by author.

/1969/KOLERS/psychology/perception/picture/shape/geometry/.

KOLERS 1969C.
Paul A. Kolers.
Some formal characteristics of pictograms.
American Scientist 57(1969)348-363.

Picture-writing (pictograms) is useful for international communication. No basic vocabulary exists for pictograms. Caricatures that emphasize distinguishing features make for easier recognition than photographs. Sometimes words are read more easily than pictures and sometimes pictures are read more easily than words, but the conditions favoring each have not been well studied. No rules now exist to guide the construction of pictorial compounds from elements, nor is enough known about the process of inference that would allow the designer to construct unambiguous compounds. Two possible solutions are outlined (1) study of inferences human readers actually draw, and (2) elimnate compounds and stick to elements. Cross-cultural confusion is minimized when pictorial elements are based on technological rather than natural objects. There are 28 references.

/1969/KOLERS/DRE/communication/writing/picture/language/.

READER'S COMMENTS -- This paper describes the primitive status of iconic communication.

KROLAK 1971.
Patrick Krolak, Wayne Felts, and George Marble.
A man-machine approach toward solving the traveling salesman problem.
Communications of the ACM 14(1971)327-34.

The traveling salesman problem belongs to an important class of scheduling and routing problems. It is also a subproblem in solving others, such as the warehouse distribution problem. It has been attacked by many mathematical methods with but meager success. Only for special forms of the problem or for problems with a moderate number of points can it be solved exactly, even if very large amounts of computer time are used. Heuristic procedures have been proposed and tested with only slightly better results. This paper describes a computer aided heuristic technique which uses only a modest amount of computer time in real-time to solve large (100-200) point problems. This technique takes advantage of both the computer's and the human's problem-solving abilities. The computer is not asked to solve the problem in a brute force way as in many of today's heuristics, but it is asked to organize the data for the humans so that the human can solve the problem easily.

The technique used in this paper seems to point to new directions in the field of man-machine interaction and in the field of artificial intelligence. There are 8 references. Abstract by author.

/1971/KROLAK/FELTS/MARBLE/RJJ/man-machine interaction/computer-aided heuristic technique/artificial intelligence/.

READER'S COMMENTS -- The paper is largely oriented to the operations research aspect of the work. However, a measurable result is obtained through the use of iconics, and this is of interest. The iconic image used is unoriginal (to wit, a map) and the hardware is not the most advanced available (a calcomp plotter). Nevertheless, the authors account for the excellent performance of their interactive system by citing the ability of a human to see all aspects of the problem and integrate them into a complete solution (ie process iconic information in parallel). They also acknowledge the importance of providing an excellent display of the salient features of the problem although in the present case the display did not require any brilliant new iconic images.

KROMHOUT 1969.
Ora M. Kromhout -- see SCHWARZ 1969.

LASKA 1970.
Richard M. Laska.
Problem solving through man-machine interaction.
Computer Decisions (April 1970) 39-42.

Through the use of an interactive graphics system, chemists are able to develop synthesis paths for complex molecules more quickly and easily than by using traditional procedures. The performance of the system is credited to the fact that the graphic system can display many alternative paths to a desired goal simultaneously and to the ability of the operator to perceive them all together and select between them. There are 4 references.

/1970/LASKA/RJJ/chemistry/display/structure/interactive/.

READER'S COMMENTS -- Another example of a practical use for interactive graphics is given: organic chemical syntheses are found rapidly and with better success than otherwise using this system. Note that the author is a magazine correspondent, and the research is that of W. Todd Wipke at Princeton University.

LEIBOWITZ 1969.
H. Leibowitz, R. Brislin, Li Perlmutter, R. Hennessy.
Ponzo perspective illusion as a manifestation of space perception.
Science 166(1969) 1174-1176.

This paper is of interest in terms of iconic communication because it documents considerable difference in susceptibility to a particular illusion. Persons raised on Guam are less able to use multiple cues that reinforce the illusion. There are 8 references.

/1969/LEIBOWITZ/BRISLIN/PERLMUTTER/HENNESSY/DRE/psychology/illusion/depth/perception/cultural/differences/.

LESK 1971, 1972.
Ann B. Lesk -- see GOLDSTEIN 1971, 1972.

LEVITAN 1960.
Eli L. Levitan.
Animation art in the commercial film.
New York: Reinhold Publishing Corporations, 1960.

The overall animation process, from conception of the story board to final production of an animated film, is presented in a clear, step-by-step easy to read way. Though the production process and some techniques may have been modernized since the book was written, the steps are essentially the same. The reader is made aware of all the complications and intervening personnel in making an animated cartoon. This is in contrast to the few people involved in computer animation, but where the final product is much less sophisticated in appearance. The book is an excellently written and illustrated introduction to the commercial animation process.

For those already in animation this book is a source of wide, general information that points to opportunities for advancement in the industry. For the advertising agency producer of commercial animation films this book should be required reading. There are no references.

/1960/LEVITAN/art/animation/cinema/.

LEWIN 1967.
Morton H. Lewin.
An introduction to computer graphic terminals.
Proceedings of the IEEE 59(1967) 1544-1967.

The purpose of this paper is to introduce the reader to some of the fundamental hardware and software aspects of typical CRT display consoles. Techniques for accomplishing display refresh are explained. The evolution of the CRT controller, from a device which simply includes a pair of digital-to-analog converters to a system which is a rather sophisticated, special-purpose hybrid processor (including analog generators and digital control logic), is developed. Means by which a user generates display processor interrupts, particularly those associated with graphic input devices, are described. The use of electronic "pens" for user interaction with a display is then explained. Finally, the software structure for a typical graphic processor is discussed from a functional point of view. The linkage between a high-level symbolic picture description and the CRT "machine language" display file, via a set of generation subroutines, is described. The calling of picture modification programs by an interrupt analysis routine is also explained. Reasons for the need of a linked-list data structure are presented. There are 22 references. Abstract by author.

/1967/LEWIN/DJM/computer/graphics/hardware/.

READER'S COMMENTS -- Concise, logical description of graphic hardware and some software considerations not burdened with minute details.

LICKLIDER 1968.
J.C.R. Licklider, Robert W. Taylor, and Evan Herbert.
The computer as a communication device.
Science and Technology (April 1968)21-31.

When computers are coupled to communication lines it changes the meaning of communication. This occurs in two ways. The first is that the communication line is used to carry data instead of voices, and thus the power of computing machinery can be brought to anyone who needs it, wherever he may be. The second is only just coming into sight, and is far more important. It is the use of the computer as a communication device in itself -- as an intermediary between people. Surprisingly, this promises to bring a new depth of intellectual interchange to the fine old art of face-to-face communication. Indeed, although authors J.C.R. Licklider and Robert W. Taylor worked face-to-face with senior editor Evan Herbert to prepare the section that follows, they foresee a day when people of similar interests will work with each other through a network of computers -- even when they are in the same room. There are no references. Abstract by author.

/1968/LICKLIDER/TAYLOR/HERBERT/education/communication/.

LIPKIN 1966.
Lewis E. Lipkin, William C. Watt, and Russell A. Kirsch.
The analysis synthesis and description of biological images.
Annals of the New York Academy of Science 128(1966)984-1012.

A tentative overall design for a system to analyze and synthesize biological image "ITSELF" is proposed. Some computer components needed to realize the system do not yet exist. Figure 14 gives an overview of the ITSELF System.

Articular properties (pattern and structure), natural complexities the biologist must study, could then be analyzed by computer. There are 16 references.

/1966/LIPKIN/WATT/KIRSCH/DRE/biological/images/programs/hardware/.

READER'S COMMENTS -- This article is concerned with the reproduction of biologic images, particularly the hardware and programs necessary to store and then re-synthesize pictures.

LOCKHEAD 1970.
G.R. Lockhead.
Identification and the form of multidimensional discrimination space.
Journal of Experimental Psychology 85(1970) 1-10.

It is proposed that people identify multidimensional stimuli as if they are loci in a multidimensional discrimination space and not by combining judgments of the separate values of each stimulus. Identification data from the 2-, 3-, and 4-dimensional stimulus sets support the model. According to this proposition, there is no theoretical limit on the number of different stimuli or objects which can be discriminated, although there is a practical limit on the number which can be identified due to the time required to learn and attach labels to each locus in the space. There are 19 references. Abstract by author.

/1970/LOCKHEAD/RJJ/perception/psychology/category/identification/.

LOUTREL 1968.
Philippe P. Loutrel.
A solution to the hidden-line for computer-drawn polyhedra.
University Microfilms, Ann Arbor, Michigan, 1968.

The hidden-line problem for computer-drawn polyhedra is the problem of determining, by means of a computer algorithm, which edges or parts of edges of a polyhedron are visible from a given vantage point.

The objective of the research described in this thesis was to find an efficient solution to the hidden-line problem. The need for an efficient solution is especially critical for on-line CRT display applications where the waiting time for the generation of a drawing must be kept to a minimum.

This thesis describes an edge classification scheme that eliminates at once most of the totally invisible edges. To test the remaining edges, called potentially visible edges, a starting point is chosen and the number of faces hiding this point, called the order of invisibility, is computed. This original order of invisibility is transmitted, with the proper modifications, to all the edges of a path originating at the starting point. A vertex test is introduced to compute the variations in order of invisibility when ever new edges from a vertex are to be included in the path. A characteristic of these paths of edges is that they are synthesized in such a way as to minimize the number of edges tested from those vertices that require a complex vertex test. If necessary, several paths of edges are generated so that each potentially visible edge is included into one and only one path.

The general hidden-line algorithm is directly extended to the case of a cluster of two or more polyhedra. It is shown that some simplifications can be made in the case where all polyhedra are convex.

A solution to the illumination problem is presented for a point source of light, with or without isotropic lighting. In the illumination problem, the object is to determine those edges of a polyhedron that are both visible to an observer at a vantage point Q and also illuminated from a point source R, R=Q.

Some illustrative examples of computer-drawn polyhedra are included, with the hidden lines removed or dashed. There are 13 references. Abstract by author.

/1968/LOUTREL/geometry/spatial/graphics/program/algorithm/.

LUMMIS 1966A.
R.C. Lummis and A.M. Noll
Simulated basilar membrane motion.
Audio/Visual Media Department, Bell Telephone Laboratories, Murray Hill, N.J.

Side-by-side stereo views of a 3-D spiral. Its exaggerated motion depicts movement of the basilar membrane of the inner ear. (11 min., silent, 16mm B. and W. film).

/1966/LUMMIS/NOLL/WHH/graphics/computer/animation/prespe-ctive/simulation/model/film/.

READER'S COMMENTS -- This computer-animated film gives a stylized stereo view of the wave propagation along the basilar membrane in response to various input signals. See also LUMMIS 1966B.

LUMMIS 1966B.
R.C. Lummis, A.M. Noll, and M.M. Sondhi.
Three-dimensional glimpse of the hearing process.
Audio/Visual Media Department, Bell Telephone Laboratories, Murray Hill, N.J.

This 5 minute, black and white 16mm computer-animated film shows the response of the basilar membrane to three input signals: sine waves of various frequencies and equal amplitude, alternating polarity pulses at three repetition rates, and the spoken word "too."

/1966/LUMMIS/NOLL/SONDHI/WHH/graphics/computer/animation/perspective/simulation/.

LYNCH 1970.
Steve Lynch and William D. Rohwer.
A two stage analysis of pictorial and verbal factors in paired associates learning.

Mimeographed paper presented Annual Meetings of the American Educational Research association, Minneapolis, March, 1970.

Paired associates learning (associating "cow" with "tie", for instance) is broken down into two stages: (1) a response learning phase, learning the responses as individual items, and (2) an associative learning phase, associating the responses to the correct experimental stimuli. Only pictures (not sentences) facilitate object learning. Both pictures and sentences promote associative learning. There are 8 references.

/1970/LYNCH/ROHWER/DRE/education/associative/learning/picture/language/.

READER'S COMMENTS -- This study provides evidence for the fundamental importance of pictures in learning.

MACCOBY 1957.
E. E. Maccoby and W. C. Wilson.
Identification and observational learning from films.
Journal of Abnormal and Social Psychology 55(1957) 76-87.

In recalling one week later material presented in films as "an ordinary entertainment film", seventh grade middle and lower class children remembered best characters and activities who matched their own sex. Boy viewers remembered aggresive content better than girls if aggression is expressed by the male character. Girls similarly remember interactive boy-girl content when expressed by females. About 60% of recognition questions were answered correctly, indicating substantial retention of material over a one-week period. There are 14 references.

/1957/MACCOBY/WILSON/DRE/learning/film/retention/.

READER'S COMMENTS -- This paper offers some evidence, incidental in terms of its main purpose, that film presentation under casual conditions leads to significant learning and that such learning effects persist at least for one week.

MACDONALD 1968A.
Stephen L. Macdonald -- see SCHADEL 1968.

MACDONALD 1968B.
Stephen L. Macdonald -- see SMITH 1968.

MACHOVER 1969.
C. Machover.
The intelligent terminal.
Extension of remarks presented at the University of Illinois "Pertinent concepts in computer graphics" Conference 30 March-2 April 1969.

This paper has discussed the definition of an "intelligent" vs a "non-intelligent" terminal and has briefly compared the instruction set and hardware configuration of two representative systems.

At the expense of hardware complexity and increased cost, the "intelligent" terminal is capable of supporting a non-flickering display and performing most housekeeping functions independent of a large central computer. Generally, these same functions can be achieved with the lower cost "non-intelligent" terminal but at the expense of significantly increased software, and much greater burden on the central computer. There are no references. Abstract by author.

/1969/MACHOVER/DJM/education/computer/graphics/interactive/hardware/design/.

READER'S COMMENTS -- An excellent contribution in terms not only of a general system of categorization, but as a thought provoking evaluation of graphic requirements.

MACKWORTH 1967.
Norman H. Mackworth, Anthony J. Morandi.
The gaze selects informative details within pictures.
Perception and Psychophysics 2(1967)547-552.

The visual fixations of 20 Ss viewing each of two pictures were measured. Each picture was later divided into 64 squares, and 20 other Ss judged their recognizability on a 10-point scale. Both measures gave high readings for unusual details and for unpredictable contours. Although they were judged to be highly recognizable, all the redundant (or predictable) contours received few fixations. Areas of mere texture scored low on both measures. The relations between fixation densities and estimated recognizability suggest that a scene may be divided into informative features and redundant regions. Not only do the eyes have to be aimed, they are usually aimed intelligently, even during the casual inspection of pictures. There are 26 references. Abstract by author.

/*KOLERS 1969A/*KOLERS 1969B/.

/1967/MACKWORTH/MORANDI/psychology/perception/pictures/.

MANKIN 1967.
Donald A. Mankin -- see CHAPANIS 1967.

MARBLE 1971.
George Marble -- see KROLAK 1971.

MARCUS 1973.
Norman Marcus -- see EGETH 1973.

MATZ 0000.
Robert D. Matz and William D. Rohwer.
Visual elaboration and comprehension of text.
Mimeo. Institute of human learning, Univ. Of California, Berkeley.
The purpose of this study was to see how much pictorial presentation facilitates comprehension of text-like passages among high SES white and low SES black fourth-graders. Visual elaboration improved performance in the black group by about

20 percent. Apparently pictorial presentation enabled the blacks to process the passages in the same manner that high SES's use without pictures. Pictorial presentation is effective only when perception of pictures reflects central conceptual activity (S's cannot simply read off correct answers from pictures). The pictures and performance by presenting material so as to convey the semantic form in which it must be processed to be understood. There are 8 references.

/0000/MATZ/DRE/elaboration/imagery/.

MEAD 1968.
Margaret Mead and Rudolf Modley.
Communication among all people, everywhere.
Natural History 77(1968)56-63.

There is need for a set of clear, unambiguous signs that can be understood by the speakers of any language and by the memebers of any culture. Glyphs, which communicate visually, are the only graphic communications device in public use. They have two advantages: (1) they do not require knowledge of any language; (2) they create a direct impact and permit immediate response. Glyphs can be image-related, concept-related, or arbitrary. It is recommended that a set of glyphs be developed to facilitate travel.

Most of the article deals with the need for a rich, second (world-wide) language. Armenian is proposed. An invented language, to express abstract concepts, is needed for research and communication among scientists. There are no references.

/1968/MEAD/MODLEY/DRE/language/picture/.

READER'S COMMENTS -- This is a good presentation of some of the pitfalls in the way of developing a set of international signs.

METZLER 1971.
Jacquline Metzler -- see SHEPARD 1971.

MICHOTTE 1963.
A. Michotte.
The Perception of Causality.
New York: Basic Books, 1963.

/*ARNHEIM 1969/.

READER'S COMMENTS -- This is an important scholarly work which deals with a fundamental problem of computer pantomimes--how to show cause and effect relationships?

MILLER 1958.
G.A. Miller and N. Chomsky.
Pattern Conception.
Proc. Univ. Michigan Symposium on Pattern Recognition, 1958 (mimeographed).

MILLER,IM 1969.
Irvin M. Miller.
Computer graphics for decision making.
Harvard Business Review 47(1969) 121-132.

This article is in two parts: I. Using graphs for decision making; II. Setting up a graphic system.

To use graphs for decision making, quantitative factors that affect business can be displayed as graphs. A set of detailed illustrations (marginal revenue and cost curves, total revenue curves, etc.) is provided. Programs allow interaction so that a second product can be evaluated assuming a first product has already been put in production. Various types of computer systems for this are discussed. In an appendix some mathematical formulas are provided (not programs) for costs, marginal costs, etc. in terms of such parameters as interest costs and plant capacity. There are no references.

/1969/MILLER,IM/DRE/computer/graphics/data/system/.

READER'S COMMENTS -- No actual programs are given.

MILLER,WC 1967.
William Charles Miller III.
An expermental study of the relationship of film movement and emotional involvement response, and its effect on learning and attitude formation.
Los Angeles: University of Southern California, Sept. 1967.

This experimental study examined the hypotheses that film motion increases audience emotional involvement, increases positive attitude response to the film and does not affect audience information retention. Other hypotheses were that the galvanic skin response (GSR) is useful for evaluating film audience emotional involvement, that audience involvement response is positively related to attitude response, and that neither emotional involvement nor attitude response is significantly related to information retention. Treatments were randomly assigned to groups of five subjects. The subjects were mostly college students. The visual portion of a 12-minute film was used for the "movement" treatment. The non-movement or "filmograph" treatment replaced each shot in the original with a single frame shown for the duration of 6 the shot. Factual narration was added to both versions so learning could be measured. Factor analysed semantic differential ratings were used to measure attitudes. Treatment groups were compared by analysis of variance. The movement groups scored significantly higher on attitude evaluation of the film but not on emotional response to the film as measured by GSR. A rise in GSR ratings indicates GSR may be a useful measure of audience response. The finding from earlier studies of no significant difference in informational learning between motion picture and film strip (filmograph) was again supported.There are 172 references. Abstract by author.

/1967/MILLER,WC/DRE/perception/psychology/.

READER'S COMMENTS -- This report turns out to be much less intriguing than its title suggests. It does emphasize once more, however, that motion is apt to be superfluous unless it has some intrinsic relation to the concepts being presented.

MILLER,WF 1968.
W.F. Miller and A.C. Shaw.
Linguistic methods in picture processing -- a survey.
SLAC-PUB-429, August 1968, Stanford Linear Accelerator Center, Stanford, California.

This paper surveys research in linguistic methods for describing and processing pictures. The rationale for a linguistic approach to picture processing is first reviewed. A general linguistic picture processing model is then presented as a basis for discussion in the survey; the central idea within the model is that of formalism for picture description. A number of research efforts are described in terms of their accomplishments, limitations, and potential usefulness. While experimental in nature, the surveyed works provide evidence that complex richly-structured pictures can be successfully processed using linguistic methods. Several common characteristics and directions for future research are indicated. There are 53 references. Abstract by author.

/1968/MILLER,WF/SHAW/IDS/picture/processing/linguistics/.

READER'S COMMENTS -- A survey of a field which is not yet ready to be surveyed. More work must be done to define the concepts before they are formalized in a math-like notation.

MINSKY 1968.
Marvin Minsky.
Semantic information processing.
The MIT Press, Massachusetts Institute of Technology, Cambridge Massachusetts, 1968.

A group of experiments directed toward making intelligent machines are collected in this book. Each of the programs described here demonstrates some aspects of behavior that anyone, except a professional skeptic, would agree require some intelligence.

Each program solves its own kinds of problems. These include: resolving ambiguities in word-meanings, finding analogies between things, making logical and nonlogical inferences, resolving inconsistencies in information, engaging in coherent discourse with a person, and building internal models for representation of newly acquired information. Each of the programs has very serious limitations in the range of situations it can handle, but the authors provide a clear perspective for viewing both the achievements and limitations of their programs.

Within its limitations the performance of each of the programs is rather good, rivaling some human performance. Thus Bobrow's STUDENT program competes, in its little domain of algebra, with the low-average high-school student, as does Evans' ANALOGY program. Raphael's and Black's programs work on somewhat more childish levels. But what is much more important than what these particular programs achieve, for each is a first trial of previously untested ideas, are the methods they use to achieve what they do.

They work by setting up goals, trying to fit data into previously acquired patterns, making models, forming and testing hypotheses, and so forth, based often on the meanings of their new and stored information. These "mentalist" terms are not to be regarded as superficial metaphors. These programs demonstrate the success of an intellectual revolution that came with the discovery that at least some mentalist descriptions of thought processes can be turned into prescriptions for the design of machines or, what is the same thing, the design of programs. There are 279 references. Abstract by author.

/*PYLYSHYN 1973/.

/1968/MINSKY/computer/artificial/intelligence/.

MINSKY 1969.
Marvin Minsky and Seymour Papert.
Perceptron -- An Introduction to Computational Geometry.
The MIT Press, Massachusetts Institute of Technology, Cambridge, Massachusetts.

It is the authors' view that although the time is not yet ripe for developing a really general theory of automata and computation, it is now possible and desirable to move more explicity in this direction. This can be done by studying in an extremely thorough way well-chosen particular situations that embody the basic concepts. This is the aim of the present book, which seeks general results from the close study of abstract versions of devices known as perceptrons.

A perceptron is a parallel computer containing a number of readers that scan a field independently and simultaneously, and it makes decisions by linearly combining the local and partial data gathered, weighing the evidence, and deciding if events fit a given "pattern", abstract or geometric.

The rigorous and systematic study of the perceptron undertaken here convincingly demonstrates the authors' contention that there is both a real need for a more basic understanding of computation and little hope of imposing one from the top, as opposed to working up such an understanding from the detailed consideration of a limited but important class of concepts, such as those underlying perceptron operations. "Computer science", the authors suggest, is beginning to learn more and more just how little it really knows. Not only does science not know much about how brains compute thoughts or how the genetic code computes organisms, it also has no very good idea about how computers compute, in terms of such basic principles as how much computation a problem should require, and what class of machine of what degree of complexity is most suitable to deal with it. Even the language in which the questions are formulated is imprecise, including for example the exact nature of the opposition or complementarity implicit in the distinctions "analogue" vs "digital", "local" vs "global", parallel" vs "serial-", "addressed" vs "associative". Minsky and Papert strive to bring these concepts into a sharper focus insofar as they apply to the perceptron. They also question past work in the field, which too facilely assumed that perceptronlike devices would, automatically almost, evolve into universal "pattern recognition", "learning", or "self-organizing" machines. The work recognizes fully the inherent impracticalities, and proves certain impossibilities, in various system configurations. At the same time, the real and lively prospects for future advance are accentuated.

The book divides in a natural way into three parts -- the first part is "algebraic" in character, since it considers the general properties of linear predicate families which apply to all perceptrons, independently of the kinds of patterns involved; the second part is "geometric" in that it looks more narrowly at various interesting geometric patterns and derives theorems that are sharper than those of Part One, if thereby less general; and finally the third part views perceptrons as practical devices, and considers the general questions of pattern recognition and learning by artificial systems.

The authors are codirectors of the Artificial Intelligence Group at Massachusetts Institute of Technology. There are 35 references. Abstract by authors.

/1969/MINSKY/PAPERT/computer/geometry/artificial/intelligence/.

MODLEY 1947.
Rudolf Modley.
Pictograms and Graphs.
Harper and Brothers 1947.

/1947/MODLEY/WHH/application/statistics/graphics/communications/.

READER'S COMMENTS -- A major effort to introduce pictographic symbols on an international scale for communicating socially significant data and facts in a form understandable by the world's population.

MODLEY 1964.
Rudolf Modley -- see BARACH 1964.

MODLEY 1968.
Rudolf Modley -- see MEAD 1968.

MORANDI 1967.
Anthony J. Morandi -- see MACKWORTH 1967.

MORAY 1970.
Neville Moray.
Attention selective processes in vision and hearing.
Academic Press, New York, 1970.

This book attempts to survey the behavioral research in

vision and hearing which throws light on how we share and divert attention, to review current theories, and to provide a guide to the relevant psychological work. Determinants of attention include intensity, extension in space, duration, emotionally-toned stimuli, repetition, suddenness, movement, novelty, association with ideas already present, accommodation of sense organs, and cessation of the stimulus. (NEISSER 1967, gives a wide-ranging review of attention research up to that time.) Chapters include; Design, analysis and conceptual framework of experiments on attention, a review of current theories of attention, auditory selection, visual selectivity, cross-model and other effects in selective perception, the sharing of attention between input and output, the time taken to switch attention, physiological research on attention mechanism, conclusions and theory.

Excerpts from the chapter on visual selectivity related to iconics will now be given. Rankings for parts of a display as to their "attention value" were found to correlate highly with the number of eye fixations on those parts of the display (p 76). The practical difficulties of experiments on vision -- preparing a run of 100 visual stimuli of known type at rates as fast as one per second, the limit of automatic slide projection, are cited. Moray looks to future use of oscilloscopes driven in line by small computers. (The abstracter sees this as possible application of computer generated movies p 81). There are gradients of "importance" in the visual field -- left hand side and top of field seem to have priority, at least in western gentiles. Visual system may approach parallel proccessing at low information rates. The author believes that valuable information about the way selected perception operates may be hidden in the vast literature on illusions, ambiguous stimuli, and the like, but despairs of this material being abstracted from that literature.

The maximum rate at which eye fixations can be made seems to be about four per second, and just over two is more usual. The author concludes (p 178) That almost nothing is known about the physiological basis of attention. Although there is not yet enough information to construct a unified theory of attention, both major approaches to visual attention postulate a discrete discontinuous time sampling as the basis for handling simultaneous messages. There are 266 references.

/1970/MORAY/DRE/theory/attention/vision/hearing/.

MORELLO 1969.
Marie W. Morello -- see SUTHERLAND,WR 1969.

MOWRER 1960.
D.H. Mowrer.
Learning Theory and the Symbolic Process.
New York: Wiley, 1960.

MUNDY-CASTLE 1966.
A.C. Mundy-Castle.
Pictorial depth perception in Ghanaian children.

International Journal of Psychology 1(1966)289-300.

Ghanaian children (N=122) aged 5 to 10, were studied. All children had attended primary school, starting at age 6. Very few children responded to the depth cues in pictures taken from Hudson's Depth Perception Test. The hypothesis that cultural stimulus is critical for the development of pictorial depth perception is supported because these children came from homes and communities where opportunities for pictorial experiences were neglible. There are 13 references.

/1966/MUNDY-CASTLE/DRE/anthropology/perception/.

READER'S COMMENTS -- Although examinations used "the vernacular language" it is not clear to what extent testing conditions may have biased the findings.

NAGELBERG 1968.
L.R. Nagelberg.
Computer graphics in electrodynamics.
Bell Laboratories Record 46(1968)70-75.

The use of computer graphics, particularly 16 mm. film animations, in electrodynamic problem result exhibition is presented. Electrodynamics gains relatively more from animation than other fields of science because of the considerable reduction in mathematical complexity due to appropriate display. Plots can be made in polar coordinates easily as well as in simple rectangular coordinates. Specific electrodynamic patterns are demonstrated and suggestions for education uses are made.

By organizing data and presenting it graphically, computers can aid engineers in understanding complex electromagnetic phenomena and aid in design of better microwave systems. A series of photos taken from computer-generated film depicts the generation of electromagnetic waves by an oscillating dipole. Because of the mathematical complexity of the laws of electrodynamics, which determine the characteristics of microwave transmission lines and antennas, design of practical systems is difficult. Computer graphics is particularly suitable for choosing parameters to optimize system characteristics. Other problems discussed include the design of a corrugated wave guide and the radiation pattern of a rectangular aperture. There are no references.

/1968/NAGELBERG/computer/animation/cinema/physics/.

READER'S COMMENTS -- Good demonstration of application of computer animation to practical problems. Example of a use where the problem truly requires graphical presentation.

NEALE 1967.
D.C. Neale -- see JENKINS 1967.

NEISSER 1967.
U. NEISSER.
Cognitive Psychology.

New York: Appleton-Century-Crofts, 1967.

NEWMAN 1969.
Colin V. Newman.
Children's size judgments in a picture with suggested depth.
Nature 223(1969)418-420.

Children at 6, 10, and 14 years were shown a perspective illusion where, if the picture is interpreted in depth, physically identical "posts' would differ in apparent size. With 6-year-old subjects the ability to give a 3-dimensional interpretation verbally did not predict susceptibility to the illusion. In fact the illusion was most marked for 6-year-olds. Results are compared with those for non-Europeans. There are 11 references.

/1969/NEWMAN/DRE/perception/development/cultural/differences/.

NICOLET 0000.
J.L. Nicolet.
Animated Geometry.
Cuisenaire Co of America, 12 Church Street, New Rochelle, N.Y., 10805.

These are 22 delightful films that reveal insights into geometrical relations without use of words or equations. 16mm black and white prints of approximately 2 minute duration each.

NIEVERGELT 1968.
Jurg Nievergelt -- see SECREST 1968.

NOLL 1966A,B.
A.M. Noll -- see LUMMIS 1966A,B.

NYGENHUIS 1972.
J. Nygenhuis -- see KATZMAN 1972.

OPHIR 1969.
D. Ophir, B.J. Shepherd and R.J. Spinrad.
Three-dimensional computer display.
Communications of the ACM 12(1969)309-310.

A stereographic display terminal has been produced using the raster display (BRAD) recently developed at Brookhaven. The system uses a rotating refresh memory to feed standard television monitors.

To produce a stereographic display the computer calculates the projected video images of an object, viewed from two separated points. The resulting video maps are stored on separate refresh bands of the rotating memory. The two output signals are connected to separate color guns of a color television monitor, thus creating a superimposed image on the screen. Optical separation is achieved by viewing the image through color filters.

The display is interactive and can be viewed by a large group of people at the same time. There are three references.

Abstract by authors.

/1969/OPHIR/SHEPHERD/SPINRAD/DJM/hardware/computer/graphics/perspective/display/interactive/color/.

READER'S COMMENTS -- Brief and clear description of a valuable and relatively inexpensive technique. Hidden line suppresion not yet programmed. Colored pictures and viewing glasses may still be available.

OWEN 1967.
D. H. Owen -- see BROWN,DR 1967.

PAIVIO 1970.
Allan Paivio.
On the functional significance of imagery.
Psychological Bulletin 73(1970)385-392.

This paper reviews the history of the imagery concept, especially with respect to its role in learning and memory. It also reviews current theory and operational approaches. There is evidence of individual differences in imagery and that these affect performance in learning, especially incidental learning. Paivio speculates that developmental changes occurring around age 8 allow changes from words to images and back -- he disagrees with Bruner's limitation of the Iconic stage to years below 8. There are 37 references.

/1970/PAIVIO/DRE/psychology/learning/memory /imagery/development/history/.

READER'S COMMENTS -- This is one of four papers (Reese, Palermo, Rohwer are the others) in a symposium.

PALERMO 1970.
David S. Palermo.
Imagery in children's learning.
Psychological Bulletin 73(1970)415-421.

The papers by Paivio (1970), Reese (1970), and Rohwer (1970) are discussed in the context of the revolutionary changes that appear to be taking place within the field of psychology. It is noted that imagery -- which these researchers have shown to be an extremely potent variable in a number of different experimental situations -- is an anomaly for behaviorism which therefore makes it difficult to provide a satisfactory theoretical account of its effects. Present theoretical efforts have failed to account for all of the data, but an hypothesis involving the leveling of figurative conceptions, which was advanced and rejected by Reese, may hold promise of accounting for these data as well as some additional data presented here. There are 41 references. Abstract by authors.

/1970/PALERMO/DRE/imagery/psychology/.

READER'S COMMENTS -- This paper discusses other papers in the Psychological Bulletin Symposium (Rohwer, Reese, Paivio).

PALLER 1970.
Alan Paller and Samuel Berger.
A map is worth a thousand printouts.
Computer Decisions (Nov 1970) 38-41.

The use of computer-assisted maps is advocated for presentation of large masses of data, and several practical suggestions for production of such maps are advanced. There are no references.

/1970/PALLER/BERGER/RJJ/graphics/application/maps/.

READER'S COMMENTS -- This paper's content is thin, but it provides a clear example of a practical use of iconics, namely the persuasive presentation of large masses of geographically-oriented data. In addition, a number of practical hints for design and production of computer maps are provided.

PAPERT 1969.
Seymour Papert -- see MINSKY 1969.

PARSLOW 1969.
R.D. Parslow, R.W. Prowse and R.E. Green, editors.
Computer Graphics: Techniques and Applications.
New York: Plenum Press, 1969.

This book is composed primarily of papers delivered at an International Computer Graphics Symposium held at Brunel University, Uxbridge, England in July 1968. It covers developments in the USA and the UK up to that time.

/1969/PARSLOW/PROWSE/GREEN/WHH/computer/graphics/engineering/application/hardware/software/.

PARSLOW 1971.
R.D. Parslow and R.E. Green, editors.
Advanced Computer Graphics; Economics, Techniques and Applications.
New York: Plenum Press, 1971.

/1971/PARSLOW/GREEN/computer graphics/applications.

PENN 1971.
Roger Penn.
Effects of motion and cutting-rate in motion pictures.
AV Communication Review 19(1971) 29-50.

This study concerns the influence of various rates of cutting on the meanings films evoke. Three types of variables were incorporated into experimental films. Subject matter (cars, people, rectangles), motion (stationary, slow, fast), and cutting rate (three constant, one accelerating, one decelerating). Groups of 10 subjects (college students) viewed each film. "Meaning" was assessed by scores from semantic differential scales and word-association production.

Rate of cutting apparently can affect meanings perceived by the audience. Fast constant rates of cutting evoke the perception of greater activity than an accelerating rate for subject matter like cars. The opposite may be true when the subject matter is people and potency is the criterion. Motion apparently evokes favorable evaluative responses. The study demonstrates that meanings can be manipulated by changing rate and type of editing in a film. Also some of the ways in which the motion of the subject matter in a film can influence perception and meaningfulness are shown. There are 12 references.

/1971/PENN/DRE/film/editing/motion/.

READER'S COMMENTS -- This study deals with issues that are of central interest to film makers, ie. What is the effect of certain editing variables on the meanings subjects see in films. There are very few studies of this kind.

PIAGET 1972.
Jean Piaget.
Physical world of the child.
Physics Today 25(1972)23-27.

The physics concepts that children develop earliest, such as "velocity" and "action", have proven to be the same concepts that have best withstood the "revolutions" in science.

Experiments have shown that the development of logical-mathematical concepts in the child parallels the development of his causal explanations. The development of these concepts follows the logical development from the fundamental to the derived eg, the move from topology to geometry.

These experiments point toward viewing the child's theorizings about causation as the manifestations of the pursuit of the objective structures that are hidden under observables. This process employs the use of those concepts currently understood to formulate theories. There are 5 references.

/*Michotte/.

/1972/PIAGET/WHH/psychology/development/children/science/causality/.

READER'S COMMENTS -- One of several papers in a special issue of Physics Today on science education of children.

PROWSE 1969.
R.W. Prowse -- see PARSLOW 1969.

PRYLUCK 1967A.
C. Pryluck and R.E. Snow.
Toward a psycholinguistics of cinema.
AV Communication Review 15(1967)54-75.

The authors assume that cinematic communication is a language, but there is no vocabulary or syntax. The use of linguistic tools and concepts may aid in studying film structure: syntactic ambiguity, semantic ambiguity, syntactic transformation, recursiveness, incongruity, and semantic or syntactic redundancy. Basic kinds of experimental manipulation to aid the analysis are channel separation, sequence change, and extraction deletion. Earlier work on these topics is reviewed. There are 56 references.

/1967/PRYLUCK/SNOW/DRE/linguistics/cinema/bibliography/.

PRYLUCK 1967B.
Calvin Pryluck.
Structural analysis of motion pictures as a symbol system.
Working Paper No. 3, Audio Visual Center, Purdue University, Nov. 11, 1967. Also AV Communication Review 16(1968 no. 4).

There are 52 references. No abstract.

/1967/PRYLUCK/education/animation/cinema/symbol/system/.

PRYLUCK 1967C.
Calvin Pryluck.
Structure and function in educational cinema.
Final Report Grant No OEG 3-7-078135-3139. Purdue University, Lafayette, Indiana, April 15, 1967.

This is a preliminary attempt toward ordering a set of propositions concerning filmic communication. Conclusions are (1) Filmic communication and language mediate the environment in different ways and are not the same except at the most general level; (2) Language and films make different demands upon the inferential capacity of the viewer; (3) Research problems for T.V., motion pictures, and filmstrips are similar.

An attempt is made to conceptualize the characteristics of filmic communication that apply in the attainment of complex educational objectives. A multi-stage process model of codification is proposed to aid comparative analysis of language and films. At level of primary coding film is specific, language is general. At level of secondary coding, films are generalized via sequencing while language is specified through sequencing. Problems in filmic communication include: (1) At the primary level, the relative contribution to meaning of coding variables (expression) and context; (2) At secondary level, the effect of serial juxtaposition of film units and the joining between picture and sound. There are 110 references.

/1967/PRYLUCK/DRE/education/communication/aural/visual/language/.

PRYLUCK 1968.
Calvin Pryluck.
Structural analysis of motion pictures as a symbol system.
AV Communication Review 16(1968)372-402.

This article proposes a consideration of the general problem of filmic communication. The author suggests as a paradigm for film analysis the method of procedure used in descriptive linguistics. In proposing an analytical model for filmic communication, the author assumes that each symbol system has a range of coding devices differing along a dimension and that the differences signal meaning. An elaborate multi-stage process model of codification is presented (p 378). A "word" and a "shot" are examples of primary coding units. An "edited picture" and a "sentence" are secondary coding units. The author notes the difference in logical structure between language and film and the general absence of devices to signal relationships between shots. When words, pictures, and music are juxtaposed one cannot assume that they fail to interact. There are 43 references.

/1968/PRYLUCK/DRE/education/cinema/symbol/system/linguistics/.

READER'S COMMENTS -- This article points to some parallels between linguistics analysis and analysis of films, but the approach does not seem to result in any non-obvious deductions.

PYLYSHYN 1973.
Zenon W. Pylyshyn.
What the mind's eye tells the mind's brain: a critique of mental imagery.
Psychological Bulletin 80(1973) 1-24

This paper presents a critique of contemporary research which uses the notion of a mental image as a theoretical construct to describe one form of memory representation. It is argued that an adequate characterization of "what we know" requires that we posit abstract mental structures to which we do not have conscious access and which are essentially conceptual and propositional, rather than sensory or pictorial, in nature. Such representations are more accurately referred to as symbolic descriptions than as images in the usual sense. Implications of using an imagery vocabulary are examined and it is argued that the picture metaphor underlying recent theoretical discussions is seriously misleading--especially as it suggests that the image is an entity to be perceived. The relative merits of several alternative modes of representation (propositions, data structures, and procedures) are discussed. The final section is a more speculative discussion of the nature of the representation which may be involved when people "use" visual images. There are 65 references.

/1973/PYLYSHYN/WHH/psychology/cognition/model/theory/.

READER'S COMMENTS -- An excellent review of the various competing theories relating to imagery and a suggestion of how these conflicting views may be synthesized into a new theory that seems consistent with recent work in artificial intelligence and the evidence of lateralization of brain function.

RABINOVITCH 1969.
M. Sam Rabinovitch (ed.)
Loops to learn by.
Brochure, National Film Board of Canada, 1969, P.O. Box 6100, Montreal 3, Quebec.

There are 100 8mm Films designed for disabled learners (children with short attention span, poor visual skills, etc.). The films encourage active participation by the learners, and are made so the child can show them himself. Teachers manuals and individual guides are available for each film. The films are grouped into six series: (1) A Look-at-it series to practice tracking, to learn form and tract it under transformations, and to provide memory and attention trainin-g;(2) A Learning-to-move series to encourage imitation of body movements, finger-and-hand movements, etc., (3) A Talk-about-it series to aid language development, (4) A series to develop strategies for problem-solving (5) A series to teach simple skills like tying a shoelace, (6) A Reading-and-writing series to give training in distinguishing letters, grapheme-phoneme correspondence, etc. There are no references.

/1969/RABINOVITCH/DRE/film/education/learning/.

REESE 1970.
Hayne W. Reese.
Imagery and contextual meaning.
Psychological Bulletin 73(1970)404-414.

Imagery facilitates paired-associate learning less than sentences in younger children, but equally in older children. Six explanations are proposed (1) Deficit in verbalization (images facilitate performance only if described verbally), (2) Defective visual memory (verbal material is remembered better than visual), (3) Production deficiency (verbal mediators are produced but not images), (4) Mediation deficiency (verbal and imaginal mediators are produced, but only verbal mediate), (5) Leveling (leveling of the image of the stimulus-response interaction into separate images of the stimulus and response destroys the stimulus-response association), (6) Failure to read (failure to observe the association depicted in the imagery condition). The author favors (6). He proposes that meaning is given by imagery, but facilitation of retention results not so much from imagery as from integrated imagery and hence contextual meaning. There are 39 references.

/1970/REESE/DRE/imagery/learning/psychology/.

READER'S COMMENTS -- This is one paper in a symposium (Rohwer, Palermo, Paivio).

REINHARD 1965.
Paul M. Reinhard.
Engineering graphics course content development study.

Final Report, NSF Grant 18762, University of Detroit, 1965.

This study was made to evaluate the role of engineering graphics in engineering education, including computer-related graphics. The role of graphics in communication was deliberately ignored. Publications to appear include a 3000-item bibliography and technical monographs giving solutions to problems in graphics that will aid the teaching of engineering. There are no references.

/1965/REINHARD/DRE/engineering/graphics/education/bibliography/.

READER'S COMMENTS -- This discusses areas for course content development in engineering graphics. The deliberate exclusion of the role of graphics in communication make it of small interest to iconics.

ROBBINS 1968A,B.
M. C. Robbins -- see KILBRIDE 1968A,B.

ROBERTS 1963.
L.G. Roberts.
Machine perception of three-dimensional solids.
Technical Report No. 315, Lincoln Laboratory, MIT, May, 1963. Reprinted in Optical and Electro optics Information Processing, Tippet et al, editors, Cambridge, Mass., MIT, 159-197

In order to enable a computer to construct and display a three-dimensional array of solid objects from a single two-dimensional photograph, the rules and assumptions of depth perception have been carefully analyzed and mechanized. It is assumed that a photograph is a perspective projection of a set of objects which can be constructed from transformations of known three-dimensional models, and that the objects are supported by other visible objects or by a ground plane. These assumptions enable a computer to obtain a reasonable, three-dimensional description from the edge information in a photograph by means of a topological, mathematical process.

A computer program has been written which can process a photograph into a line drawing, transform the line drawing into a three-dimensional representation, and finally, display the three-dimensional structure with all the hidden lines removed, from any point of view. The 2-D to 3-D construction and 3-D to 2-D display processes are sufficiently general to handle most collections of planar-surfaced objects and provide a valuable starting point for future investigation of computer-aided three-dimensional systems. There are 13 references. Abstract by author.

/*PYLYSHYN 1973/*ROBERTS 1966/

/1963/ROBERTS/WHH/computer/perception/spatial/program/picture/.

READER'S COMMENTS -- This remarkable doctoral dissertation introduced a set of mathematical ideas that are eminently applicable to describing perceptual processes. By using homogeneous coordinates to describe vertices, edges, and surfaces of solid objects, perspective transformations are linearized and, hence, the parameters needed to describe the scaling, translation, and rotation of the solid object as well as the viewpoint of the viewer relative to the object can be inferred by ordinary least squares to minimize the discrepency between the prototype object and its perspective view (such as represented by a photograph). Although homogeneous coordinates are a well-known part of the mathematical theory of projective geometry, their use to describe objects in the visual field has unfortunately been ignored despite their great usefulness for this purpose.

ROBERTS 1966A.
Lawrence G. Roberts.
The Lincoln wand.
Proceedings of the Spring Joint Computer Conference (1966) 223-227.

An ultrasonic position sensing device in the form of an ultrasonic receiver the size of a pen is described. The device receives two pulsed signals from four transmitters and can be used for two or three dimensional localization in a working space of 4X4X6 feet. Computer utilization time is approximately 1 percent. There are four references.

/1966/ROBERTS/DJM/computer/graphics/hardware/.

READER'S COMMENTS -- Useful device described including a good indication of relative merits of item-pointing versus position-pointing capabilities and the adaptation of a position-pointing device as an item-pointing device. Advantages of 3D to go through large bodies of data is well taken. Adequate mathematical explanation of position sensing geometry and error analysis.

ROBERTS 1966B.
Lawrence G. Roberts.
A graphical service system with variable syntax.
Communications of the ACM 9(1966) 173-175.

/1966/ROBERTS/DJM/computer/graphics/software/system/.

READER'S COMMENTS -- Lucid description of design requirements for and examples of capability for a Graphic Service System. Deals effectively with both structural and mathematical relations.

ROBERTS 1966C.
Lawrence G. Roberts.
Homogeneous matrix representation and manipulation of N-dimensional constructs.
The Computer Display Review, C.W. Adams Associates, Inc., Cambridge, Mass., 1966.

The theory of projective geometry is idealy suited for the description of spatial objects since by describing the vertices, edges and surfaces of such objects by their homogeneous coordinates, various transformations (such as scaling, translation, rotation, anisotropic stretching, and perspective projections) are all representable by linear transformations. Hence, familiar least-square methods may be invoked to find the transformation that converts a given primitive prototypical shape (such as a unit cube) into the visual image as seen by a viewer from some unknown viewpoint. The power of this method was demonstrated by the author in his remarkable thesis (ROBERTS 1963).

This brief summary extends the material presented in his thesis. It is a sketchy outline of a number of very important and useful results that call for a fuller, tutorial treatment to make these methods available to psychologists and others who could benefit form using the mathematical formalism in modeling visual phenomena.

/*AHUJA 1968/.

/1966/ROBERTS/WHH/geometry/theory/spatial/invariance/.

READER'S COMMENTS -- Although so sketchy as to be difficult to comprehend, this summary of some of the important properties of homogeneous coordinates and their application is worth studying. These ideas deserve much wider use and application than they have thus far received.

ROBERTS 1967.
L.G. Roberts.
Conic display generator using multiplying digital-analog converters.
IEEE Transactions on Electronic Computers 16(1967) 369-370.

A simple waveform generator for display systems has been designed on the basis of homogeneous coordinate mathematics. This generator will draw points, lines and general conic sections. The fundamental waveform used is the parabola. Circles, ellipses, and hyperbolas are merely perspective transformations of the basic parabola, which is represented by the parametric vector $T=(t^2,t,1)$. The design of the homogeneous conic generator is based upon the assumption that a multiplying digital-to-analog decoder can be built economically. The decoder produces an output voltage proportional to the product of a ten-bit digital number and a positive reference level; it must maintain 0.1 Percent accuracy up to about 100 kHz. In its simplest form the generator would contain 11 decoders. Allowing subpicture scaling and centering requires 14; adding cubics requires 18; and most complicated system, with three-dimensional cubics with a final perspective transformation as well as the two-dimensional transformation, requires 34 decoders. There are 4 references.

/1967/ROBERTS/DJM/computer/geometry/display/graphics/.

READER'S COMMENTS -- Description of desirable function generator for complicated forms based on homogeneous coordinates. Prototype not actually available at time article was written.

ROE 1951.
Anne Roe.
A study of imagery in research scientists.
Journal of Personality 19(1951)459-470.

This important paper reports evidence from apioneering study of the personalities of research scientists as related to vocation. Visual thinking is strongly correlated with vocation. Biologists and experimental physicists reported strong reliance on visual imagery in their thinking whereas psychologists and anthropologists appeared to rely more on verbal and symbolic modes of thought.

In considering whether possession of a particular mode of imagery (verbal or visual) leads a person to a particular vocation or, conversely, working in a vocational field develops particular modes of thought and imagery, the author has evidence for the former. She also finds that "subjects who do not follow the imagery pattern most typical for their own group are also somewhat less like their colleagues in their work and personalities." This difference seems to consist largely in manner of approach to problems. Life histories furnish some indication that there were also differences in interests (as shown by spontaneous activity) in high-school and early college days. There is also a high correlation of imagery type with the occupation of the subject's father.

/1951/ROE/WHH/research/personality/imagery/verbal/differences/.

READER'S COMMENTS -- A fascinating, suggestive paper that suggests that the appropriatness of iconic modes of communication may be vocation dependent.

ROHWER 0000.
William D. Rohwer -- see MATZ 0000.

ROHWER 1967.
William D. Rohwer, Jr.
Social class differences in the role of linguistic structures in paired-associate learning.
Final Report Project 5-0605, Contract No. OE-6-10-273, University of California, Berkeley, November 1967.

/1967/ROHWER/DRE/linguistic/learning/differences/.

ROHWER 1970A.
William D. Rohwer, Jr.
Images and pictures in children's learning.
Psychological Bulletin 73(1970)393-403.

A number of experiments are reviewed that pertain to the issue of the role of imagery in children's learning. The studies reviewed include those concerned (A) With properties of learning items, (B) With properties of the elaboration of learning items, and (C) With properties of elaboration instructions. The relevant evidence is viewed developmentally, and it is concluded that the capacity for deriving optimal benefit from verbal modes of representation emerges earlier in children's learning processes than the capacity for deriving optimal benefit from pictorial modes of representation. Some educational implications of imagery research are discussed. There are 29 references. Abstract by author.

/1970/ROHWER/JWW/education/imagery/picture/perception/paired-associates/

READER'S COMMENTS -- Author's conclusions run counter to the commonly accepted theories, eg Bruner's. His conclusions are summarized as follows,

A. The probability that imagery will be evoked in younger children is lower than that probability for older children.

B. The capacity for deriving profit from imagery representation develops later than the capacity for deriving profit from verbal representation.

C. The capacity of imagery storage to facilitate learning is contingent upon the simultaneous storage of an accompanying verbal representation of the same event, and that such simultaneous storage is more probable for older than for younger children.

ROHWER 1970B.
William D. Rohwer.
Mental elaboration and learning proficiency.
Final Report, OEO Contract no. 2404, 119-138.

Visual forms facilitate learning in eight year olds but not four year olds. Relevant data presently avaiable suggest that more proficient learners (college students) are characterized by more autonomous elaborative activity than less proficient learners (school children). Others have reported from data obtained in post learning interviews that the frequency of reported elaborative activity increases significantly with grade level.

The author proposes that the iconic mode of presentation is not primitive, but indeed follows or parallels the verbal in development. There are no references.

/1970/ROHWER/DRE/learning/elaboration/development/.

READER'S COMMENTS -- Only a small part of this paper is relevant to iconics but the hypothesis counter to Bruner's on the sequence of verbal and iconic development is especially important.

ROMNEY 1967.
Gordon Romney -- see WYLIE 1967.

ROSENFELD 1969.
Azriel Rosenfeld.
Picture Processing by Computer.
Academic Press 1969.

No abstract. There are 452 references.

/1969/ROSENFELD/computer/graphics/.

ROVNER 1967.
Paul D. Rovner.
The LEAP language and data structure.
Technical Report DS-5554, Lincoln Laboratory, MIT, Lexington, Mass., November 1967.

One problem of current interest in computer science is the processing of relational structures. Considerable effort has been directed toward developing a flexible, efficient system for recording and using complex relations between items of information. This development has been guided by two basic needs:

(A) a convenient way for a human to express his instructions on how to manipulate a relational structure, and

(B) an efficient way to represent a relational structure inside the computer. This work is an extension of the hash-coded associative processing schemes.

The paper is divided into two sections, corresponding to two areas of development. The first section describes the high-level computer language, LEAP, proposed for associative processing. The implementation of the relational structure, which included provisions for secondary storage, is described in Section II. The language and data structure are independent but do seem to be quite well matched. There are 11 references. Abstract by author.

/*SUTHERLAND 1969/

/1967/ROVNER/computer/language/data/structure/.

SALOMON 1968.
Gavriel Salomon and Richard E. Snow.
The specification of film attributes for psychological and educational research purposes.
AV Communication Review 16(1968) 225-244.

This paper points out that effects due to media must be defined as interaction effects between media and learners. Further attributes of media should be defined that are psychologically relevant. No data are presented but an unpublished experiment is reviewed. The experiment used criteria of cue-attendance and hypothesis generation with two versions of a film. An interaction was found between film type and performance at task, although it is not clear how it was measured. There are 35 references.

/1968/SALOMON/SNOW/DRE/media/learning/psychology/education/.

READER'S COMMENTS -- This paper is mostly discursive.

SAMUELS 1970.
S.J. Samuels.
Effects of pictures on learning to read, comprehension and attitudes.

Review of Educational Research 40(1970)397-408.

In its yearly summary of investigations related to reading, the Reading Research Quarterly reports nearly 400 studies. Surprisingly, only a fraction of the studies were concerned with pictures or illustrations. This review is a summary of those studies in which researchers have investigated the effects of pictures on (A) learning to read, (B) comprehension, and (C) attitudes. In addition specific suggestions for needed research are included. To delineate the area for review, preference was given to those studies in which pictures were used as adjuncts. Pictures are considered adjuncts if the text can be comprehended or the objects of the lesson fulfilled when the pictures are removed.

1. The bulk of the research findings on the effect of pictures on acquisition of a sight-vocabulary indicate that pictures interfere with learning to read.

2. There was almost unanimous agreement that pictures, when used as adjuncts to the printed text, do not facilitate comprehension.

3. In the few studies done on attitudes, the consensus was that pictures can influence attitudes.

Should pictures be used as adjuncts to printed text? The answer depends on the objectives. If the objective is to pro-mote acquisition of a slight vocabulary, the answer would seem to be "no". If the objective is to facilitate comprehension, the answer is less definite. Although the research, in general, does not show that pictures aid comprehension, neither does it show that it hinders comprehension. Much research still needs to be done on the effect of pictures on attitudes.

One argument for including illustrations with basal readers and with other books used to teach reading is that attractive pictures may help a child develop positive attitudes toward reading. Learning to read is a difficult task for many children, and it is possible that attractive pictures which accompany the text may make the task of learning to read a bit more pleasant. Unfortunately, not a single study has come to this author's attention which can answer the question to the effect of pictures on attitudes towards reading. A study to answer this question would be easy to design and should be done. If a study such as the one suggested here were to be done, and if it were found that presence of attractive pictures made reading more enjoyable, the educator might find himself on the horns of a dilemma; that is, whether to keep pictures out of books to facilitate learning to read or to include pictures to build favorable attitudes toward reading. A solution which might satisfy both objectives might be to keep pictures out of the child's text and to give the teacher an appropriate series of large and colorful pictures for each story. The teacher might then show and discuss each picture as she builds a background for the story. When the children actually read, the pictures would be put away. Still another solution might be to include pictures in the student's book, but to organize the book so that pictures and text were separated in such a manner that the pages with printed text would be free of pictures. There are 30 references.

/1970/SAMUELS/DRE/education/pictures/learning/reading/bibliography/.

SARNO 1968.
Frank Sarno.
The polygraphics software package--a summary of its features.
Proceedings of 7th UAIDE Annual Meeting (1968) 402-409.

/1968/SARNO/computer/graphic/software/.

SAUVAIN 1969.
R.W. Sauvain.
A teachable pattern describing and recognizing program.
Pattern Recognition, Pergamon Press 1(1969) 219-232.

The paper discusses an adaptive pattern recognition program that learns to recognize coded line drawings, and to describe the structure of the pattern by giving the hierarchical organization of its subparts, and the spatial relationships between them. Emphasis is on mechanisms that allow learning (directed by feedback from a human trainer), and on the methods of abstracting, storing, and retrieving chunks of graphic information for use in subsequent pattern recognition and description. Some similarities to the perceptual process in humans are noted. There are 14 references. Abstract by author.

/1969/SAUVAIN/computer/model/adaptive/artificial/perception/.

SCHADEL 1968.
Jay A. Schadel and Stephen L. Macdonald.
Three-dimensional input for computer graphics.
Technical Report 1-1, ARPA Order 829, Program Code No. 6D30, University of Utah.

This paper states the need for three-dimensional input for architectural work using computer graphics. The paper consists of two sections. The first section deals with laser scanning; X, Y, being a mechanical scan, and Z being a modulated laser source timing the reflected laser beam. The second section explains the use of photogrammetry for X, Y, Z information. (Photogrammetry is the science of measuring using photographs.) Examples are given comparing old methods of ground survey with photogrammetry. There are 11 references. Abstract by author.

/1968/SCHADEL/geometry/computer/grahics/picture/spatial/.

SCHROEDER 1969.
M.R. Schroeder.
Images from computers and microfilm plotters.
Communications of the ACM 12(1969) 95-101.

Digital computers are widely used for the processing of information and data of all kinds, including the pictorial information contained in photographs and other graphical representations. Efficient conversion facilities for putting graphical information into the computer and retrieving it in graphical form are therfore much needed. One of the most commonly employed devices for obtaining permanent graphical output from digital computers is the microfilm plotter. Regrettably, present models have no provision for producing images with a continuous gray scale or "halftones." In this note several programming techniques are described for obtaining halftone pictures from a microfilm plotter under the control of a digital computer. Illustrative examples of several methods are given. There are no references. Abstract by author.

/1969/SCHROEDER/DJM/computer/graphics/software/image/halftone/.

READER'S COMMENTS -- Elegant system for adding the ability to add halftone output to computer graphics. Good illustrations of results of technique and clear explanations of programming techniques.

SCHWARCZ 1968.
Robert M. Schwarcz -- see SIMMONS 1968.

SCHWARTZ 1969.
Judah L. Schwartz -- see KAHNE 1969.

SCHWITZGEBEL 1962.
R. Schwitzgebel.
The performance of Dutch and Zulu adults on selected perceptual tasks.
Journal of Social Psychology 57(1962)73-77

When a series of visual and cognitive tasks were presented to Dutch and Zulu subjects in South Africa, Zulus were significantly less accurate in estimating figure size and passage of time. The greatest difficulty was associated with locating a simple 2-dimensional figure embedded in a more complex design. The subjects of both races were males, 19 to 24 years old, with 4-5 years of education, who spoke both Dutch and Zulu. There are 20 references.

/1962/SCHWITZGEBEL/DRE/anthropology/visual/perception/.

READER'S COMMENTS -- The effect of tester's race and language on performance is not discussed. The results might differ with a Zulu tester testing Zulus.

SECREST 1968.
Don Secrest and Jurg Nievergelt.
Emerging Concepts in Computer Graphics.
New York: W.A. Benjamin, Inc., 1968.

This book delineates the basic problems in the field of computer graphics, with special attention to those problems still unresolved. It came out of a 1967 University of Illinois Conference supported by NSF. There are 97 references. Abstract by author.

/1968/SECREST/NIEVERGELT/computer/graphics/.

SEGAL 1971.
Sydney Joelson Segal (editor).
IMAGERY: Current Cognitive Approaches.
Academic Press, New York, 1971.

This volume presents five different empirical approaches to the study of imagery, all of which stem from a cognitive theoretical framework by T.X. Barber, B.R. Bugelski, R.N. Haber, A. Paivio, and S.J. Segal. Using many new experimental techniques, the papers range from discussions of the brief image or icon which serves as the source of storage in short term memory to considerations of global behavior changes, including hallucinatory imagery under the influence of drugs and hypnotic states. The role of the image in verbal learning and the relationship of the image to both the sensory and cognitive aspects of cognition are also considered.

Topics discussed include: a theoretical approach to imagery and language; eidetic imagery, the icon as image, and the experimental measurement of this icon; study of the image by empirical-behavioristic methods; relations and analogies between image and percept; comparison of imagery in normal, hypnotic, and drug-induced states.

The book will be valuable to psychologists in the fields of cognition and perception, to researchers in visual perception, and to graduate students in these areas.

/*PYLYSHYN 1973/.

/1971/SEGAL/WHH/psychology/cognition/imagery/.

SEGALL 1963.
M.H. Segall, D.T. Campbell and M.J. Herskovits.
Cultural differences in the perception of geometric illusions.
Science 139(1963)769-775.

This paper reviews methods and findings of a 6-year cross-cultural study of 14 non-European samples of children and adults and of 3 European groups concerning perception of 4 illusions. Using the psychophysical method of constant stimuli, the authors found cross-cultural differences in illusion susceptibility and systematic variation in these differences over two classes of illusion figures. The non-Europeans were less susceptible to the Muller-Lyer and Sander Parallelogram illusion and more or less susceptible (non-European broke into two sub-groups) to the two horizontal-vertical illusions. The authors interpret cross-cultural differences in terms of ecological and cultural factors in the visual environment (rectangularity in highly carpentered environments and vertical lines open-flat-terrain environment).

/1963/SEGALL/campbell/herskovits/DRE/anthropology/illusions/cultural/differences/.

READER'S COMMENTS -- This paper summarizes a large amount of cross-cultural data and gives details of "environmental" explanations for susceptibility to illusions.

SEGALL 1966.
Marshall H. Segall, Donald T. Campbell, and Melville J. Herskovits.
The Influence of Culture on Visual Perception.
New York: the Bobbs-Merrill Company, Inc., 1966.

The study reported is a joint psychological-anthropological one concerning the role of culturally determined experience in visual perception. Data were collected from 15 societies using stimulus materials based upon five geometric illusions. It was found that on both the Muller-Lyer and the Sander parallelogram illusions the European and american samples made significantly more illusion-supported responses than the non-Western samples. On two horizontal-vertical illusions, the European and american samples had relativley low scores, with many of the non-Western scoring higher. The authors emphasize the bidirectionality of the findings -- non-Westerners being less susceptible to illusions like the Muller-Lyer and more susceptible to horizontal-vertical. Westerners see a "carpentered world" and have experience with two-dimensional models. Non-Westerners see broad horizontal vistas. There is clear-cut demonstration of cross-cultural differences in the data, not the same for all illusions. There was failure to find corroboration in age-trend data. There are 170 references.

/1966/SEGALL/CAMPBELL/HERSKOVITS/psychology/anthropology/perception/cultural/illusion/.

READER'S COMMENTS -- This study is methodologically sophisticated.

SEIBERT 1965.
Warren F. Seibert -- see SNOW 1965.

SEVERIN 1967A.
Werner Severin.
The effectiveness of relevant pictures in multiple-channel communications.
AV Communication Review 15(1967)386-401.

Six message conditions (audio, print, audio plus print, audio plus pictures, audio with unrelated pictures of the same category) were tested with 7th grade students. The measure was recall. Multiple-channel modes were superior to single channel when relevant cues are summated across channels, and are inferior when irrelevant cues are combined. Audio with related pictures was significantly better than audio with print. Audio with print was not better than print alone. Irrelevant picture condition were poorest. There are 20 references.

/1967/SEVERIN/DRE/communication/aural/visual/pictures/memory/.

SHAW 1968.
A.C. Shaw -- see MILLER,WF 1968.

SHAW 1969.
Alan C. Shaw.
Parsing of graph-representable pictures.
Technical Report No. 69-34, April 1969, Dept. Of Computer Science, Cornell University.

This paper describes a syntax-directed picture analysis system based on a formal picture description scheme. The system accepts a description of a set of pictures in terms of a grammar generating strings in a picture description language; the grammar is explicitly used to direct the analysis or parse, and to control the calls on pattern classification routines for primitive picture components. Pictures are represented by directed graphs with labelled edges, where the edges denote elementary picture components and the graph connectivity mirrors the picture component connectivity; blank and don't care "patterns' allow the description of simple relations between visible patterns. The bulk of the paper is concerned with the picture parsing algorithm which is an N-dimensional analog of a classical top-down string parser, and an application of an implemented system to the analysis of spark chamber film. The potential benefits of this approach, as demonstrated by the application, include ease of implementation and modification of picture processing systems, and simplification of the pattern recognition problem by automatically taking advantage of contextual information. There are 21 references. Abstract by author.

/1969/SHAW/linguistics/picture/representation/system/.

SHEPARD 1966.
Roger N. Shepard.
Learning and recall as organization and search.
Journal of Verbal Learning and Verbal Behavior 5(1966)201-204.

/1966/SHEPARD/verbal/learning/recall/.

SHEPARD 1967.
Roger N. Shepard.
Recognition memory for words, sentences, and pictures.
Journal of Verbal Learning and Verbal Behavior 6(1967)156-163.

/1967/SHEPARD/psychology/memory/word/picture/differences/.

SHEPARD 1971.
Roger N. Shepard and Jacquline Metzler.
Mental rotation of three dimensional objects.
Science 171(1971)701-703).

The time required to recognize that two perspective drawings portray objects of the same three-dimensional shape is found to be (i) a linearly increasing function of the angular difference in the portrayed orientations of the two objects and (ii) no shorter for differences corresponding simply to a rigid rotation of one of the two-dimensional drawings in its own picture plane than for differences corresponding to a rotation of the three-dimensional object in depth. Abstract by author.

/1971/SHEPARD/METZLER/JWW/perception/perspective/rotation/experiment/.

SHEPARD 1973.
R.N. Shepard and G.W. Cermak.
Perceptual-cognitive explorations of a toroidal set of free-form stimuli.
Cognitive Psychology 4(1973) 351-377.

SIMMONS 1968.
Robert F. Simmons, John F. Burger, and Robert M. Schwarcz.
A computational model of verbal understanding.
Proceedings Fall Joint Computer Conference 33(1968) 441-456.

The authors believe that the long-term goal for computational linguistics is to provide ways for computers to deal effectively with natural languages in such applications as question-answering, stylistic and content analysis, essay writing, automated translation, and so on. This requires models for linguistic structures and also models for verbal understanding and verbal meaning. A general purpose language-processing system, Protosynthex III, is described. It works on a sentence-by-sentence basis. The model includes a linguistic component that is composed of a lexicon and syntactic and semantic systems. The formal conceptual structure includes inference rules, a limited quantificational capability, and a logical structure of relations that are definable by properties for use in inference procedures. An important next step is to expand the model from one of sentence understanding to one suitable for larger discourse structures. The program is in LISP 1.5. There are 31 references.

/1968/SIMMONS/BURGER/SCHWARCZ/DRE/computer/linguistics/.

SMITH 1968.
Max J. Smith, Stephen L. Macdonald, C. Stephen Carr.
Space-form: computer aided design for architecture.
Architectural Research Information Processing System, Technical Report 1-2, University of Utah, September, 1968.

The chief aim of this paper is to describe a process of design involving the computer. "Space-forms' are used as graphical computer input. These 3-dimensional forms are used by the designer as building blocks to design at every scale, up to the eventual placement of the building in the context of its surroundings. Some descriptive maneuvers are being programmed and debugged but are far from complete and have not been tested. The total system (not available now) will include: 1) a space-form design system, 2) a data storage and retrieval system, 3) a structural design system, 4) a quantity and cost analysis system, 5) various building systems (mechanical, electrical, etc.), 6) A survey input system, 7) numerical control output for models or components. The ultimate system would work something like this: when the design is complete it will be stored on tape. A contractor could call the design on his own console, by rotation, scanning, sectioning, etc. He could then order specs as required for his purpose, and get quantity and cost data for bidding and ordering. All changes and bookkeeping would be automatic. There are no references.

/1968/SMITH/MACDONALD/CARR/DRE/computer/design/architecture/display/.

READER'S COMMENTS -- This is a proposal for rendering of 3-dimensional forms using a simple small set of basic forms. It is noteworthy in its contrasting approach to that found in the "random" shapes proposed by psychologists. No trials or other actual work implementing this proposal have as yet been carried out.

SNOW 1963.
Richard E. Snow.
The importance of selected audience and film characteristics as determiners of the effectiveness of instructional films.
Final Report, USOE Grant 712142, Audiovisual Center, Purdue University, Lafayette, Ind. 1963.

This report contains 2 studies.

(1) This research concerns personal characteristics of the learner in studies of instructional films vs. conventional presentation. Fourteen audience characteristics (attitudes, "emotional stability", etc.), Different levels of previous knowledge, and film vs. live were factors in study design. Seven learner variables interacted with mode of presentation (see Table 24, P. 115). Live presentation led to better scores (immediate recall) than films for students with little previous knowledge of physics and unfavorable attitudes toward films, for example. The pattern of findings is not simple, nor is it clear to what extent the findings are functions of the particular film used.

(2) This research explores individual film production variables. (Audio-visual complexity, audio iconicity, video iconicity, temporality, artificiality, internal repetition). A study of these and learner variables leads to the following hypotheses.

(A) verbal learning is facilitated by auditory presentation of complexity while non-verbal learning is facilitated by visual presentation,

(B) long films, or films perceived as long, are less effective instructionally than live presentations of the same material in the same time interval;

(C) visual realism is not necessarily desireable;

(D) film literacy is a learning set developed through film viewing practice, which facilitates learning from artificial film presentations;

(E) internal film repetition is conducive to increased learning. Visual realism is apparently inversely related to student achievement. There are 68 references.

/1963/SNOW/DRE/education/visual/verbal/learning/.

READER'S COMMENTS -- The number of statistically significant findings in Study 1 is not large compared to the number of tests made. The variables identified in Study 2 suggest that films can be categorized multidimensionally to aid in studying instructional effects.

SNOW 1965.
Richard E. Snow, Joseph Tiffin, and Warren F. Seibert.
Individual differences and instructional film effects.
Journal of Educational Psychology 56(1965) 315-326.

In an investigation of instructional treatment by learner-varible interaction, 437 college Ss were divided between filmed and live physics lecture demonstrations. Immediate- and delayed-recall criteria were applied. Using prior knowledge of physics and 14 other learner characteristics as independent moderator variables, a series of 2 X 3 X 3 unweighted means analyses indicated that attitude toward instructional films, ascendancy, responsibility, numerical aptitude, verbal aptitude, past experience with entertainment films, and past use of college Library instructional films interacted significantly with instructional treatments, primarily on the immediate-recall criterion. Prior knowledge of physics modified most of these effects. Attitudes toward entertainment films and toward physics, emotional stability, sociability, total personality self-evaluation, academic achievement, and unspecified past experience with instructional films did not interact with instructional treatments. There are 14 references. Abstract by author.

/*HUGGINS 1968/.

/1965/SNOW/TIFFIN/SEIBERT/education/physics/verbal/visual/learning/.

SNOW 1967.
Richard E. Snow -- see PRYLUCK 1967A.

SONDHI 1966.
M.M. Sondhi -- see LUMMIS 1966B.

STACEY 1970.
B. Stacey -- see JAHODA 1970.

STEGER 1971.
Joseph A. Steger -- see SHEPARD 1971.

STENSON 1966.
Herbert H. Stenson.
The physical factor structure of random forms and their judged complexity.
Perception and Psychophysics 1(1966) 303-310.

This study relates the perceived complexity of 20 random forms to their physical factor structure. Ten principal axes, accounting for 94 per cent of the total variance of 24 physical measures, were rotated using the Varimax criterion. Factor scores for each form were correlated with the complexity ratings of the forms by each of 11 Ss. A single factor accounted for most of the variance in the complexity ratings. This factor was best described by four physical measures: the number of turns in the form, the length of the perimeter, the perimeter squared to area ratio, and the variance of the internal angles of the form. There are 7 references. Abstract by author.

/1966/STENSON/psychology/perception/physical/shape/complexity/.

STEVENSON 1969.
Harold W. Stevenson and Alexander Siegel.
Effects of instructions and age on retention of filmed content.
Journal of Educational Psychology 60(1969) 71-74.

Boys and girls (N=472) in grades 3-7 were shown an 8-minute dramatic skit filmed in sound and color. Prior to seeing the film Ss were told to atten to (A)auditory material, (B)visual material, or (C)both. On posttest, 31 questions of multiple choice or Yes-No type, were given. Auditory information showed better retention than visual (about 2 items) under all instructions. Across grades, visual questions got a little better (1 item over 5 grades) and auditory information got a little worse (1/2 item over 5 grades). There are 4 references.

/1969/STEVENSON/SIEGEL/DRE/education/psychology/visual/auditory/interaction/memory/.

READER'S COMMENTS -- It is not clear whether visual cues (colors,etc.) bear any significant relation to content or plot. If visual cues are irrelevant to story line of movie, one would not expect them to be retained. One question, for example, was: what color was the wife's apron?

STEWART 1965.
J. C. Stewart.
An experimental investigation of imagery.
Unpublished Ph.D. Disseration, University of Toronto, 1965.

These experiments were designed to investigate use of imagery by adults of a narrow "range of intelligence but wide range in imaging ability judged by two spatial manipulation tests".

Experiment 1 concerned two paired associate lists, one with pictures of common objects, the other with words. Pictures were learned more quickly by the whole group but high-imagers learned in fewer trials than low imagers.

Experiment 2 investigated recognition of pictures and words. Results again shcw pictures superior, but difference favoring high imagers over low imagers still appears.

Experiment 3 studied a free recall of three word lists of varying vividness. Low imagers surpassed high imagers, but vividness helped all subjects.

Some evidence suggests low imagers more frequently coded a picture as a word, and high imagers coded words as pictures. These experiments document the adult use of imagery, contradicting earlier speculations that imagery is unimportant for adults. There are 100 references.

/1965/STEWART/DRE/imagery/.

READER'S COMMENTS -- This study indicates that imaging ability can influence adult performance.

STRANDBERG 1969.
Twila E.Y. Strandberg.
An evaluation of three stimulus media for evoking verbalizations from pre-school children.
Unpublished M.S. Thesis.
Eastern Illinois University Library.

This study was designed to determine the relationship between the stimulus used to evoke verbal language samples from children and measures of sentence length, grammatical complexity and number and variety of words uttered. Three stimulus media were used to evoke samples from 30four and five-year-old subjects. Ten subjects were assigned to each of the three media in such a manner as to counter-balance the groups for age and sex. The contents of the three stimulus media were toys, color photographs of the toys and twenty-second single concept films of the objects represented by the toys. The language samples were evoked following a practice session using a standardized procedure and verbal directives. No limit was placed on the amount of verbalization from the subjects for each of the nine items within each medium. Extraneous verbalizations, however, were not included in the final analysis. Throughout the study the examiner variable was held constant. All samples were tape recorded, transcribed and analyzed by the examiner.

Four language measures were applied to the samples: (1) the length-complexity-index; (2) mean-length-response; (3) total number of words; and (4) number of different words.

The results of the statistical analyses revealed no significant differences among the three stimulus media for both the length-complexity-index measures and the mean-length response measures. However, both toys medium and the film medium were significantly higher than the pictures medium in total number of words and number of different words but they were not significantly different from each other.

The measures obtained in this study are compared to the results of three previous studies. Two of these studies employed the same language measures but used different stimuli to obtain language samples from four- and five-year-old subjects. The third study used the same stimuli, language measures and procedures for evoking samples as the present study but with mentally retarded subjects. These comparisons indicate that while measures of average sentence length are not affected by different stimuli, measures of grammatical complexity and sentence length and measures of amount and variety of words vary significantly with changes in stimuli. There are 31 references.

/1969/STRANDBERG/DRE/education/language/.

STROMBERG-CARLSON 1965.
Stromberg-Carlson Corp.
S-C 4020 Computer Recorder Information Manual.
Stromberg-Carlson Corporation, San Diego, Calif., 1965, 37 Pages.

The S-C 4020 microfilm recorder is described in both its internal function and off- and on-line configurations. The CHARACTRON (reg. Trademark) CRT, cameras available and types of output are covered in the most detail. There are no references.

/1965/STROMBERG-CARLSON/DJM/computer/graphics/animation/.

READER'S COMMENTS -- Good, basic introduction to what is the standard recorder for graphics, including animation. A newer model, the S-C 4060 is now available. Little programming information is included in the manual.

SUTHERLAND,IE 1963.
I.E. Sutherland.
Sketchpad: a man-machine graphical communication system.
Lincoln Laboratory Technical Report no. 296, Jan. 30, 1963, Massachusetts Institute of Technology. Also, Proceedings of the Spring Joint Computer Conference 22(1963)329-346

The Sketchpad system uses drawing as a novel means of communicating with a computer. The system contains input, output, and computation programs that enable it to interpret information drawn directly on a computer display. It has been used to draw electrical, mechanical, scientific, mathematical and animated drawings; it is a general-purpose system. Sketchpad has shown the most usefulness as an aid to the understanding of processes, such as the motion of linkages, which can be described with pictures. Sketchpad also makes it easy to draw highly repetitive or highly accurate drawings and to change drawings previously drawn with it.

Several simple and very widely applicable facilities have been discovered and implemented. They provide a subpicture capability for including arbitrary symbols on a drawing, a constraint capability for relating the parts of a drawing in any computable way, and a definition copying capability for atomic constraints. When combined with the ability to point at picture parts given by the demonstrative light pen language, the subpicture, constraint, and definition copying capabilities produce a system of extraordinary power. The system is useful in a wide range of applications (including animation). There are 22 references. Abstract by author.

/1963/SUTHERLAND/SMZ/computer/graphic/interactive/design/system/.

READER'S COMMENTS -- The report is a comprehensive review of an early attempt at developing a man-machine system using only drawings (and related control functions) for communication. The report discusses the applications of Sketchpad, its strengths and weaknesses, as well as its basic design. Though some parts are less than clearly described, all the design questions- data structure, light pen function and use, coordinate systems, transformations, utility design programs, use of recursive functions, copying and constraining drawings are all answered. It is interesting to read how each problem was solved, and the reasoning behind each solutions, since these problems are common to all graphical displays attempting to communicate intelligently with humans.

SUTHERLAND,IE 1966.
Ivan E. Sutherland.
Computer graphics.
Datamation (May 1966) 22-27.

No abstract. There are 11 references.

/1966/SUTHERLAND/computer/graphics/.

SUTHERLAND,WR 1966.
W.R. Sutherland.
On-line graphical specification of computer procedures.
Lincoln Laboratory Technical Report No. 405, May, 1966, Massachusetts Institute of Technology.

A promising area of application for recently developed computer graphics techniques is computer programming. Two important considerations in using an interactive graphics system for drawing programs are (1) the form of a pictorial programming notation and (2) methods for making a computer execute the program once drawn. These topics are discussed in the context of an experimental graphical programming system running on the Lincoln Laboratory TX-2 Computer. This system uses a block notation for programs and can execute the drawn program with an interpreter. Improved graphical input languages for drawing programs and program notations which combine appropriate features of pictorial and written languages are needed before applications in this area are practical. The benefits to be expected from a graphical approach to programming include (1) automatic documentation, (2) debugging assistance, and (3) natural expression of parallel processes. There are 37 references. Abstract by author.

/1966/SUTHERLAND/SMZ/computer/graphic/program/interactive/system/.

READER'S COMMENTS -- The report is of peripheral interest to computer animation because the communication of pictures to and from the computer is involved. The pictures on the graphics terminal are a two dimensional source language for the computer not for the human operator. Conceptually it may be better to program by flow charts, but the practical problems of defining primitive operations, creating a small part of the program at a time, and inefficient interpretation by the computer diminish the positive effects of the system. The report mentions the problems and also suggests future work in the area. One possible application of the system is to specify both a program and its data pictorially. This could lend itself to animation in a crude way.

SUTHERLAND,WR 1969.
William R. Sutherland, James W. Forgie, and Marie W. Morello.
Graphics in time-sharing: a summary of the TX-2 experience.
Proceedings Spring Joint Computer Conference 34(1969)629-636.

The summary is well done and focuses on both the hardware and software of the TX-2 computer with its graphics terminals. Hardware dependent data, structures, a time-shared scope signal generator, and a tablet instead of a light pen are the major hardware peculiarities. A section of the article mentions the various planned and unplanned applications which were tried on the system. Included, of course, was the computer animation system of R.M. Baecker. A critique of all experiences follows. The statement is made that for interactive computer graphics to be successful the programmer must have access to convenient programming tools, and these programs must run well in their operating environment. Most of the experiments with the system were qualified successes and there are lessons to be learned from them. There are 23 references.

/1969/SUTHERLAND/SMZ/computer/graphic/interface/system/.

TALBOT 1971.
P.A. Talbot, J.W. Carr, R.R. Coulter, and R.C. Hwang.
Animator: an on-line two-dimensional film animation system.
Communications of the ACM 14(1971unications of the ACM 14(April)251-259.

TAYLOR 1966.
Calvin W. Taylor and Frank E. Williams (editors).
Instructional media and creativity.
The Proceedings of the Sixth Utah Creativity Research Conference held at Torrey Pines Inn, La Jolla, California. New York: John Wiley and Sons, Inc. 1966.

No abstract. There are 206 references.

/1966/TAYLOR/WILLIAMS/education/media/.

TAYLOR 1968.
Robert W. Taylor -- See LICKLIDER 1968.

THOULESS 1933.
Robert H. Thouless.
A racial difference in perception.
Journal of Social Psychology 4(1933)330-338.

This paper is the source paper on phenomenal regression. The tendency of some viewers to perceive objects in their "real" rather than "perspective" form, that is, circular object in perspective is elliptical but some subjects , particularly non-western persons, perceive it with major and minor axes equal. In testing British and Indian subjects the author finds significantly greater phenomenal regression in the Indians. The author advances this as a explantion of the absence of perspective and shadows in Oriental art. There are 4 references.

/1933/THOULESS/DRE/anthropology/perception/cutural/differenc-es/.

READER'S COMMENTS -- This is an important paper historically for anthropological studies of visual perception.

TIFFIN 1965.
Joseph Tiffin -- see SNOW 1965.

TRAVERS 1967.
Robert M.W. Travers.
Research and theory related to audiovisual information transmission.
U.S. Department of Health, Education and Welfare Office of Education Contract No. 3-20-003 (Distributor -- Western's Campus Bookstore, Western Michigan University, Kalamazoo, Michigan, 49001).

No abstract. There are 332 references.

/*PRYLUCK 1967C/*HUGGINS 1968/*DWYER 1970/

/1967/TRAVERS/education/aural/visual/communication/.

TUNG 1962.
Tze-Hsiung Tung -- see DACEY 1962.

UHR 1961.
Leonard Uhr and Charles Vossler.
A pattern-recognition program that generates, evaluates, and adjusts its own operators.
Computers and Thought, McGraw-Hill Book Company, Inc., 1963.

This article takes a new approach to pattern recognition programs by developing one that can adapt to almost any set of input patterns and quickly become proficient in them. It constantly improves its ability to make discriminations between similar patterns, but can handle widely diverse patterns as well.. There are no references.

/1961/UHR/VOSSLER/TWB/computer/pattern/artificial/perception/.

READER'S COMMENTS -- Article is from a book which covers all aspects of pattern recognition which is also in bibliogra-phy.

UHR 1963.
Leonard Uhr.

Pattern recognition -- computers as models for form perception.
Psychological Bulletin 60(1963)40-73.

This paper is a rather wordy review of various attempts at using machines for pattern recognition. There is insufficient detail to gain much insight into the various procedures cited without a reasonable familiarity with references. If one already has a more than cursory understanding of the references then this paper is of dubious value. There are 159 references. Abstract by author.

/1963/UHR/DGW/computers/artificial/perception.

UHR 1965.
Leonard Uhr.
Feature discovery and pattern description.
Manuscript reprint.

Through the use of an example program, Uhr shows that a program that cannot learn new patterns on its own will never develop good discrimination ability over a general set of patterns. There are 16 references.

/1965/UHR/TWB/computer/artificial/pattern/perception/.

VOSS 1969.
J.R. Voss -- see KADANOFF 1969.

VOSSLER 1961.
Charles Vossler -- see UHR 1961.

WALL 1971, 1972.
Sally Wall -- see EGETH 1971, 1972.

WARNOCK 1968.
John E. Warnock.
A hidden-line algorithm for half-tone picture representation.
Technical Report 4-5, ARPA order 829, Program Code Number 6D30, University of Utah.

The purpose of this paper is to consider the problem of producing two dimensional halftone image representations of objects described in 3 space. In discussing the main problem of the removal of hidden surfaces in a picture representation, the motivating philosophy of a particular approach is closely examined, and a description of a possible implementation of this appooach is described. The advantages of the scheme are also outlined in the paper. Problems in black and white, also color, are dealt with. There are no references. Abstract by author.

/1968/WARNOCK/computer/graphics/spatial/representation/color/halftone/surface/.

WARNOCK 1969.
John Warnock.

A hidden surface algorithm for computer generated halftone pictures.
Ph.D. Thesis, June 1969, RADCTR-69-249, Technical Report 4-15, ARPA order 829, Program Code Number 6D30.

The application of computer graphics to problem solving has increased over the past few years. The representation of data in the form of line drawings, graphs, charts, diagrams and line plots has been explored extensively. This paper addresses itself to some new techniques used to solve problems associated with extending the power of computer graphics to include black and white, and color shading. In particular it presents a new method for converting data describing three-dimensional objects into data that can be used to generate two-dimensional halftone images. It deals with some problems that arise in black and white, and color shading. There are 8 references. Abstract by author.

/*ERDAHL 1969/.

/1969/WARNOCK/computer/graphics/shading/color/hidden/surface/.

WATT 1966.
William C. Watt.
Morphology of the Nevada cattle brands and their blazons: part one.
National Bureau of Standards Report, No. 9050, Washington, D.C., Feb. 10, 1966.

The Nevada cattle brands and their blazons offer an unusually tractable example of a highly codified system of associated pictorial sources and descriptions thereof. A "syndeictic" analysis of this brand-and-blazon system is presented and related to the general problem of analyzing such systems by means of techniques drawn from linguistics. There are 23 references. Abstract by author.

/1966/WATT/linguistics/picture/syntax/.

WEINER 1966.
Donald Weiner -- see HUGGINS 1966.

WEINER 1968.
Donald D. Weiner and S.E. Anderson.
A computer animation language for educational motion pictures.
Proceedings of the Fall Joint Computer Conference 33(1968)1-317.

/*WEINER 1971/.

/1968/WEINER/ANDERSON/computer/language/animation/education/movies/.

WEINER 1971.
Donald D. Weiner.
Computer animation--an exciting new tool for educators.

Institute of Electronic and Electrical Engineers Transactions on Education E-14(1971)202-209.

A tutorial paper on computer animation that answers the following questions:
1) What is computer animation and how did it begin?
2) Who is active in this area?
3) What is the present state of the art?
4) How is computer animation accomplished in a batch-processing environment?
5) What is the role of interactive graphics?
6) What are some of the special techniques that are being developed?
7) How does one get started?
Extensive bibliography includes 129 references and 86 computer-animated films.

/*HUGGINS 1971/.

/1971/WEINER/WHH/computer/education/animation/movie/bibliography/.

WEIZENBAUM 1963.
J. Weizenbaum.
Symmetric list processor.
Communications of the ACM 6(1963)524-536.

A list processing system in which each list cell contains both a forward and a backward link as well as a datum is described. This system is intended for imbedding in higher level languages capable of calling functions and subroutines coded in machine language. The presentation is in the form of FORTRAN programs depending on only a limited set of "primitive" machine language subroutines which are also defined. Finally, a set of field, particularly character, manipulation primitives are given to round out the system. There are 4 references. Abstract by author.

/1963/WEIZENBAUM/computer/language/data/structure/system/.

WHITE 1961.
W. White.
The computer as a pattern generator for perceptual research.
Behavioral Science 6(July 1961)252-259.

This paper previews the capabilities of the computer in perceptual research by relating things that have been done already. He shows five areas of applications.

1. Pattern recognition and threshold determination by showing a reversed random walk on the points comprising the figure 5.

2. Pattern metamorphosis into another by a "directed" walk of the points comprising the pattern into the desired new pattern.

3. Movies showing the kinetic depth effect of a rigid rotation of a bent wire pattern which is projected onto the picture plane.

4. Studies of projecting a hyperspace into a space of lower dimensionality , eg Hypercube projected into 3-space and then the corresponding 3-space object projected into the 2-space picture plane.

5. Statistically defined bar patterns determined by distributions based on different parameters were generated and used to study the grouping phenomenon. There are 7 references.

/1961/WHITE/JWW/psychology/psychophysics/perception/patterns/computer/.

READER'S COMMENTS -- Many of the possible applications suggested in this article have been or can be accomplished via available computer-graphic programs. The use of computers to design perceptual experiments with motion and binocular vision capabilities has not yet been fully exploited by the psychophysicists in their research.

WICKELGREN 1970.
W.A. Wickelgren and P.T. Whitman.
Visual very-short-term memory is nonassociative.
Journal of Educational Psychology 84(1970)277-281.

An array of alternating black digits and letters on a white background was presented for 50 msec. at an illumination of 20 ftl., followed by a dark delay varying from 200 msec. to 2 sec., followed by a black test character on a gray background (500 msec. at .11 ftl.), followed by 4 sec. in which Ss recalled the character appearing to the right of the position of the test character. A visual very-short-term memory trace was obtained for six out of eight Ss, decaying with a time constant of about 2 sec. All Ss had a substantial "nondecaying" tachistoscopic memory component. Presenting as a test character the character which had actually appeared in that position in the preceding array did not enhance recall at any delay for any S by comparison to presenting a dummy character in that position. Thus, tachistoscopic memory is nonassociative. Memory for position is by an ordered, two-dimensional array of locations, not by associations between character representatives. There are 8 references. Abstract by author.

/1970/WICKELGREN/WHITMAN/DRE/psychology/visual/memory/.

WILLIAMS 1966.
Frank E. Williams -- see TAYLOR 1966.

WILLIAMS 1970.
Clarence M. Williams and John L. Debes.
Proceedings of the First National Conference on Visual Literacy.
New York, Pitman Publishing Co., 1970.

This is a record of a 1969 conference of psychologists, educators, elementary and secondary school teachers, representatives of companies making film supplies and others. For the most part 57 short papers presented by those attending the conference are discursive and anecdotal. There is little if any content of the kind one finds in the scientific literature. Most of the papers are concerned with increasing the use of visual materials in education and with the ways to bring this about. The collection of papers has little to do with iconics per se.

/1970/WILLIAMS/DRE/education/visual/literacy/.

WILLIAMS 1972.
Robin Williams.
A general purpose graphical language.
Report TR-403-21. Department of Electrical Engineering, New York University.

This paper describes a high-level extensible language for graphical applications. The language allows the user to define new data types and new operations with these data types to suit his needs and to simplify subsequent programming. Data types and operations for creating three-dimensional polyhedral objects and for specifying transformations on objects are presented, together with examples. Objects can also be created and edited by working interactively. Motions and other functions, such as interpolation, that apply to an object can be described in the written language or interactively as well. Thus the user can create his own suitable environment and depending upon the nature of the problem, he can work with a written language, or interactively, or he can work with a combination of both methods. Such flexibility at a high level should simplify the use of graphical facilities. There are 21 references.

/1972/WILLIAMS/NDB/computer/graphics/language/interactive/.

WILSON 1957.
W.C. Wilson -- see MACCOBY 1957.

WILSON 1969.
Glen D. Wilson.
Modular computer programs for image-processing and manipulation.
AFCRL-69-0234, May 1969, Physical and Mathematical Sciences Research Papers, No. 381, Bedford, Massachusetts, L.G. Hanscom Field.

Several members in a family of modular image-processing computer programs are described. A data structure useful for image-processing is defined. Modular programs, under control of an executive program, operating within this data structure are described as vaulable tools for image-processing research. The modular programs, designated Micro Instructions, perform such operations as image sampling, storage, erasure, coding, isodensity plane extraction, framing, graphing, etc. There are 3 references. Abstract by author.

/1969/WILSON/computer/graphics/system/hardware/.

WINOGRAD 1972.
T. Winograd.
Understanding natural language.
Cognitive Psychology 3(1972) 1-191.

/*PYLYSHYN 1973/.

WOBER 1966.
Mallory Wober.
Sensotypes.
Journal of Social Psychology 70(1966) 181-189.

WOHLWILL 1965.
J. F. Wohlwill.
Texture of the stimulus field and age as variables in the perception of relative distance in photographic slides.
Journal of Experimental Child Psychology 2(1965) 163-177.

The perception of relative distance in the third dimension, on the basis of photographic stimulus fields, was studied in children in Grades 1, 4, 8, and 9, and college adults. Photographic slides were made of stimulus fields constructed to represent four degrees of texture density and degrees of regularity of patterning of the texture elements. For each texture the perceived midpoint of a standard distance was determined by means of an adaptation of the method of constant stimuli. The results indicated a general error of underestimation (underconstancy), which decreased somewhat with age. At all age levels this error decreased as texture density increased, but there was no significant interaction between age and texture. Regularity of patterning produced less consistent effects, though there was an over-all increase in constancy from the least to the most regular pattern. The judgments showed a high degree of consistency at all age levels, pointing to the advantages of this type of psychophysical method for the study of perceptual judgments in children. There are 12 references. Abstract by author.

/1965/WOHLWILL/DRE/depth/perception/development/.

READER'S COMMENTS -- This study presents futher evidence for the early asymptoting of perceptual development linked to ambient vision.

WORTH 1968.
Sol Worth.
Cognitive aspects of sequence in visual communication.
AV Communication Review 16(1968) 121-145.

Visual communication is the transmission of a signal, perceived primarily through visual receptors, from which content or meaning is inferred. Film is an expecially good medium for studying visual communication.

Elements differing in four parameters (image, space, motion, and time) are put into sequence by the film-maker and from this the viewer infers meaning. Brief sequences of film composed of abstract forms (circles, triangles, etc.) were tested with subjects aged 13 to 19 using a semantic-differential scale. The hypothesis that sequence will be more critical with similar elements than with dissimilar elements is confirmed in a preliminary way. Other studies suggest that persons from other cultures form sequences differently. There are 23 references.

/1968/WORTH/DRE/visual/communication/cognition/.

READER'S COMMENTS -- This is an attempt to provide a theoretical context for analysis of meaning in films or other visual communicators. It draws from no other body of theory and does not appear very useful.

WYLIE 1967.
Chris Wylie, Gordon Romney, David Evans, and Alan Erdahl.
Half-tone perspective drawings by computer.
Technical Report 4-2, ARPA order 829, Program Code number 6D30, Nov. 14, 1967, (Revised 2/12/68 in accordance with ARPA Technical Report 4-3). University of Utah.

This paper is a brief description of an algorithm for the creation of two-dimensional, half-tone pictures of perspective projections of three-dimensional objects. Only the visible surfaces are displayed; all hidden surfaces are erased. This process is independent of the orientation of the object. The inclusion of half-tone shading was considered important because the illumination of an object gives a viewer much information about the three-dimensionality of the object. A FORTRAN IV program is working on a Univac 1108. Preliminary results indicate that this approach is not only possible, but practical for complex objects. Processing time is small and storage requirements are very compact. There are 5 references. Abstract by author.

/*WARNOCK 1969/*APPEL 1968B/

/1967/WYLIE/ROMNEY/EVANS/ERDAHL/computer/graphics/perspective/halftone/.

ZAJAC 1966.
Edward E. Zajac.
Computer graphics -- notes from course EE 398.
Polytechnic Institute of Brooklyn.

No abstract. There are no references.

/1966/ZAJAC/WHH/computer/graphics/geometry/hidden-lines/program/.

READER'S COMMENTS -- These unpublished notes contain an excellent introduction to the use of vector notation for dealing with objects in 3-dimensions. This material contains sample FORTRAN subroutines for shading and other operations.

ZIMMERMAN 1967.
Luther L. Zimmerman.

On-line program debugging -- a graphical approach.
Computers and Automation (Nov 1967).

The GBUG graphical debugging system is described. The person doing the debugging wants particularly quick response. The graphic display has speed, the ability to present large amounts of data with each response and has the CRT-light pen interface for efficient two-way conversation. The programming was done such that the IBM 2250 terminal could be used to exhibit memory location contents, change register contents and provide several types of dumps. All memory presentations are in hexadecimal. There are no references.

/1967/ZIMMERMAN/DJM/computer/graphics/interactive/software/.

READER'S COMMENTS -- Concise presentation of a useful tool.

ZUSNE 1970.
Leonard Zusne.
Visual Perception of Form.
Academic Press, New York, 1970.

This reference offers a systematic source of information on all aspects of static, two-dimensional visual form as it has been conceptualized historically and until the recent past. The comprehensive bibliography appended to the book contains 2583 items.

/1970/ZUSNE/WHH/psychology/visual/perception/bibliography/.

ZWARG 1972.
Stephen M. Zwarg.
Sailing: an example of computer animation and iconic communication.
Proceedings of the Spring Joint Computer Conference 40(1972)-1005-1015.

This paper describes an example of computer animation -- a short film on sailing -- which uses visual imagery in the communication process. The paper also describes the author's activities in producing the film. The film, of a sailboat racing around a course, demonstrates sailboat aerodynamics. It consists entirely of visual symbols. The author discusses some of the principles and practices that may contribute to film success in communicating abstract ideas--especially those relating to motion and timing. There are 11 references.

/1971/ZWARG/DRE/physics/iconic/film/sailing/demonstration/.

INDEX

Library of Congress Cataloging in Publication Data

Huggins, William H
Iconic communication.

1. Symbolism (Psychology)—Bibliography. 2. Idols and images—Bibliography. 3. Communication—Psychological aspects—Bibliography. I. Entwisle, Doris R., joint author. II. Title.
Z7204.S9H83 016.0015 73-8130
ISBN 0-8018-1528-2